Make Yourself

By Gillian Smith

Published in 2021 by
GREEN CAT BOOKS
19 St Christopher's Way
Pride Park
Derby
DE24 8JY

www.green-cat.co

FIRST EDITION
Copyright © 2021 Gillian Smith
All rights reserved.
ISBN: 978-1-913794-18-7

All rights reserved.

No part of this publication
may be reproduced in any form or by any
means without the prior written permission of
the publisher.

This book is sold subject to the conditions that shall not, by way of trade or otherwise, be lent, resold, hired out, or otherwise circulated without the publisher's prior consent in any form of binding other than that in which it is published and without a similar condition including this condition being imposed on the subsequent purchaser.

DEDICATION

To every person that has ever felt they weren't good enough, simply because they were not like the rest. To every person who has suffered in silence, at the fear of being judged. To every person who has ever felt alone, when there was no need to be, I write this for you.

And to every person who has stood by a loved one, and patiently waited for them to find themselves, to love themselves, you are what makes it all worth it.

MAKE YOURSELF

CONTENTS

	Introduction	1
1	Outside of the Circle	3
2	Path to Popularity	16
3	The Beginning of the End	33
4	Summer Lovin'	47
5	Darkness and Light	60
6	A Whole New World	76
7	A Boy Called Tom	90
8	Forever Bound	102
9	The Darkness Returning	110
10	Let's Get This Party Started	119
11	The Cost of Living	130
12	The Day the World Ended	135
13	Down the Rabbit Hole	141
14	Home Alone	150
15	He Loves Me, He Loves Me Not	158
16	It Never Rains, It Pours	174
17	A Whole New World V2.0	184
18	Driftwood	201
19	The Calm Before the Storm	217
20	The Trick is to Keep Breathing	227

MAKE YOURSELF

Introduction

When I was a little girl, my all-time favourite movie was Walt Disney's Dumbo. Even at four years old, I would cry throughout most of the film. During the scene where Dumbo visits with his mother in prison and she rocks her baby to sleep, then, and even now, I am inconsolable. A complete wreck. I don't quite remember, but my mum tells me now that the tears would start to flow before anyone had even hit play on the remote. Yet, for reasons I didn't quite understand, it was still my favourite. On a four-year-old level, I guess I just liked the cute doe-eyed elephant and the funny little mouse. But on a deeper level, Dumbo is a story that aspires us to be anything we want to be. It teaches us that no matter what cards life deals you, no matter where you come from, or what you have been through, you are capable of being anything that you let yourself be. I'm not sure that Dumbo was ever intended to be an emotionally educational venture to teach young children about strength and determination, but for me, that's what it was. And even if I didn't quite understand it at the time, for me, it was a life lesson, the first of many.

When we are children, we are taught that the world is a shiny, happy place and that when we hold out our hands and ask nicely for the things that we want, we will be given them. We are taught that, at the end of the rainbow there is a smiling leprechaun with a funny green hat, waiting to dish out his pot of gold to the person lucky enough to find him. We are reassured by loving parents, that there is no monster under the bed, and that no one is coming to get us.

Even as a child, I never believed it. I always knew there was a darkness in the world that no one wanted us to know about or to admit, and it isn't surprising to me that my strongest memories of my childhood, are those in which I am pretending to be someone else, somewhere else. As a teenager, I had no trouble seeing the world for what it really was, cruel and unyielding. During the most trying time of anyone's life, I found myself living in a world which I hated, and which I felt hated me. Every day, I was fighting my way through darkness and self-hatred; whilst all the time, dealing with even bigger life problems - being a teenage girl. Friendship, betrayal, first loves, lost loves, temptation and dreams of escape. I blamed myself for not being strong enough to cope, for not being 'normal' enough to fit into the world in the way which everyone else seemed to be able to. I grew to hate myself, sinking into a deep depression, until eventually I got lost there and thought I would never get out, that there was no point in trying.

But sometimes, you need to live in darkness, before you can see the light. Before you can see the difference between night and day. And sometimes, you need to hit rock bottom to make you realise which direction you need to walk in, once you get back on your feet again.

We all need to learn to fall, in order to learn how to get back up again. And if we can't or won't remember all the ways in which we've fallen, then we can't remember all the times we've gotten back up again. And it is getting up, again and again, that will make us stronger, and remind us why we need to stay strong. It is how we make ourselves.

Chapter 1 – Outside of the Circle

"There is nothing like returning to a place that remains unchanged to find the ways in which you yourself have altered" – Nelson Mandela.

When I was a kid, my greatest achievement in life was in my short-lived career as an actress. Each year, our primary school drama teacher Mrs Stewart, would choose one class in the school to perform as a group at the Aberdeen Arts Centre. It was a great honour to be chosen. Schools from all over Aberdeenshire took part in the event, each taking turns to do a group performance, on stage, in front of an audience of hundreds of students and teachers from other schools. For most, a terrifying experience. But for me, it was my chance to shine. For one reason or another, Mrs Stewart favoured our class, and we got to perform at the Arts Centre several times during primary school. But the year that I knew I was going to be star, Mrs Stewart had chosen for our performance, an interpretation of *The Bat's Choice;* a story of self-realisation in which a bat needs to decide whether to join the animals, or the birds, before deciding, just to be a bat instead.

It was a silent performance that would rely on miming and movement to convey the story of the confused bat and the animal groups. The animal group consisted of an array of different animals – foxes, rabbits, deer, and the leader of the animal group – the bear. The leader of the birds, of course, the eagle. My best friend and all-time rival, Hannah was the bear. She could be the bear - because *I* was the eagle. It may not have been the main part, but it was by far the most majestic. The day of our final performance was the best day of my life.

After sneaking onto the stage behind the drawn curtain, we waited nervously in the darkness for the stage to light up, presenting us like trophies in front of what felt like millions of people. My heart pounded in my chest as I stood poised on top of my soap box. Leader of the birds, my place was higher than anyone else's. This was my moment, and I was ready for it. I heard my classmates around me chitter nervously as they waited for the curtain to rise. *Amateurs.*

The class drew in a collective breath in anticipation as the curtain lifted and the music started to flow. *Here we go.* Still poised in position, ready and waiting, I watched as the spotlight followed the bat around the stage, as he flitted indecisively amongst the other players. First, he flew to the animals, investigating each one before crossing the stage to the birds. He crisscrossed between the two groups, not able to agree where to settle. Defeated by his own lack of identity, he faded out of the spotlight, back into the shadows at the back of the stage. The stage went black.

When the spotlight reappeared, this time it was on me. I stood silently; arms wrapped around my body in what I imagined to be a bird-like shape. I stood high, two foot above the rest of my classmates who were gazing up at me, worshipping my authority as their leader. Slowly and purposefully, I unravelled my arms from across my body, allowing them to flow gently through the air. I imagined them stretching out into perfectly sculpted wings, gentle but strong feathers spanning from my fingertips, ready to propel me off my soapbox as if I was standing on the cliff edge of a canyon. I could see the deep plunge beneath me, but I was ready, knowing that I could trust my wings to carry me. I raised my head up, pushed my chest out and raised my arms strong above my shoulders, allowing the audience to revel in the power held within my wingspan. With all the grace I could gather, I leaped off my soapbox and imagined myself soaring through the wind like an eagle, the canyon spreading wide below me as I sailed effortlessly over it. I closed my eyes and felt the cold air of the sky on my face as I floated between the other birds on the ground, gently greeting each one as I passed my royal subjects. The spotlight followed my every move as I soared around the stage and I could feel a million eyes on me all at once. Although I had rehearsed it a thousand times, each time I did, my feet took me different directions around the stage. I didn't have to think about where I was trying to go or what I was trying to achieve, my body just knew. The eagle didn't have to choose a path, because it was already laid out in front of it. It didn't have to choose a side to be on, because it already had a place in the world. All of the attention, all of the focus in the entire room, was on me. As I soared across the stage, I became that eagle. For just a few minutes, I didn't have to be myself, I could be somebody or something else, something better. I could be an eagle. Free and majestic, respected and feared, loved and admired. I wished I could stay that eagle forever. I was too young to know it at the time, but it was the first time I ever really wanted to be something, someone else, other than myself.

In real life, my whole world revolved around my best friend, Hannah. Everyone had that one person. That one person who you thought would be your best friend until the very day you died. That one person who knew all your secrets, who was closer than anyone else, so close, you convinced yourselves that you could read each other's minds, just because you were so 'on the same wavelength'. In my case, it was my best friend, and the most important person in the whole world, Hannah. I always felt that I never quite fit anywhere. That I was always just hanging on, always on the outside. But with Hannah, everything just slotted into place. I didn't need anybody else but her.

Hannah was the type of person who you either loved greatly or hated with a passion. I loved her greatly. In the beginning, I thought she was one of kind. She was loud and bold and more fun than anyone I'd ever met before. She was always looking to start a new adventure, which although happened rather often, usually ended in tragedy, or embarrassment. Our favourite weekend pastime when we were kids, was to transform ourselves into private investigators, catapulting the sleepy little village where we lived into a world full of strange and suspicious events.

The adventure I remember the clearest started one afternoon while walking home after an afternoon at the local swimming pool. Across the street from the pool was, what we believed to be an abandoned car garage. The garage had been there for as long as we could remember. It had been vacant for years, so when we heard voices trailing out from the abandoned grounds, it was only natural that we would feel the need to investigate. A steep, grass hill acted as a wall around the premises and provided a perfect cover to allow us to get closer, without putting our lives in any real danger. We crawled silently up the slope and crouched hidden in the long grass like soldiers on a mission. We positioned ourselves high enough to get within earshot but low enough to keep hidden, just like the professionals we would surely one day become. The men behind the hill were arguing, but as we shuffled *silently* into position, their stealth hearing picked up on our presence and one man warned the other to stay quiet. As they tried to listen for us, fear grew tight in our stomachs and we lay silent and motionless in the grass.

'Come on, let's get outta here!' one man said, before shifting nervously towards one of the cars and getting in.

The car sped off up a country trail that led off from the entranceway, a road which, as far as we were aware, led to nowhere but suspicion.

A huge wave of relief washed over us both as we relaxed in our own silence. Thanks to Hannah's vivid imagination, together with her excellent powers of persuasion, suddenly, the men were criminals. What other explanation could there possibly be? We remained glued into position in the grass for the next hour, discussing what we had discovered. What were they so worried about us hearing? Why did they leave so suddenly? What were they arguing about? What were they doing in an abandoned car lot in the first place? If they were criminals, then what was their crime? Were they harbouring stolen goods? Cars, TV's, jewellery, people? We decided that it was our duty, as detectives, not to let such criminal activities seep into this safe, sheltered, little town. *Our* safe, sheltered little town. We agreed that we would have to make several more visits to the garage in order to carry out vital surveillance on the property, allowing us to gather enough evidence to take to the police, making us local heroes (obviously). Medals of honour, here we come! But not tonight. Darkness was looming and we had enough images of dangerous criminals circling our over-active imaginations for one day. Besides, it was almost dinnertime. Our mission was set to begin at 11 a.m. tomorrow morning.

We walked home, growing more and more anxious with each step.

We talked excitably of the danger we would be in if we got caught spying, comparing ourselves to James Bond and the deadly situations he ends up in whenever a mission goes sideways. We imagined being held captive by the men (who were becoming increasingly dangerous and who, by this point, were now serial murderers), escaping to the police, collecting our medals of honour, and saving the whole town. The fame, fortune - and all by the age of ten. This would be our greatest adventure yet.

Hannah and I met the next morning, armed with notepads and the highest technology available to us, disposable cameras. We were ready for action. We synchronised our watches and split up to cover more ground, arranging a meeting point nearby. While Hannah lay low on the hill as look-out, I threw caution to the wind and volunteered (I think) to sneak round the back of the hill and into the car lot, ready to investigate the mysterious grounds of the old garage. I carefully approached the entrance, peeking slyly around the hill to make sure no one was around. There was a large warehouse in the middle, which looked like it might collapse into a pile of rubble if the wind caught it the wrong way. It was locked. The rest of the yard was busy with cars in different states of disrepair. Some were write-offs, rimmed with thick orange rust. Some with broken windows and missing doors. Some of these cars must have been almost as old as me. The spaces between the rust buckets were occupied by newer cars, given away by their significant lack of rust, all windows and doors present. I wondered why anyone would keep these wrecked cars. Surely, this was the evidence we were looking for. The men must be stealing parts from the old cars and selling them illegally. They must be running the garage in secret and replacing perfectly good parts in the new cars with the old, rusted ones from the write-offs, forcing their trusted customers to keep coming back and keep paying more and more. Who would do such a thing?

As I started to walk around the back of the warehouse, it grew more and more suspicious. There were snakes of burnt rubber lacing the ground and a tall metal drum standing alone in the middle of the yard, which looked like it had been set on fire. *That must be where they burn the bodies.* My imagination let the smell of burning seep into my senses. Consumed with trying to analyse my surroundings, I tripped and went flying towards the ground. I quickly found my feet and composed myself, knowing that Hannah would be sniggering to herself in the grass. When I looked behind me to see what I had tripped over, I saw a long, thick chain laying in a pool of liquid. The orange rust seeped into the liquid like blood. *What they used to tie people up before killing them.* I felt terror rise up through my stomach and into my throat, as images flashed before my eyes of the dangerous consequences we talked excitably about the night before. Fear flooded my senses and excitement melted away; the close reality of danger was not so much fun. I decided that it was time to get out as quickly as I could. I bent down to take the chain with me - evidence. It was heavy and strong, and I couldn't help imagining having to try to break through it. I would be completely helpless. *What would James Bond do?* I wondered. Suddenly, a voice boomed behind me, making me jump.

'Oi! What you doing in here?'

I spun around and almost lost my balance when I realised I was looking up at one of the criminals we had seen yesterday. I froze. Shackled by the same fear that took over my insides only moments ago, when I found the chain that they obviously used to tie up trespassing children, armed only with a notepad and a camera. He towered tall above me and I could see the rough texture of his shaven head. He reminded me of a prison inmate that I had seen in the movies. His body bulged from his grease-stained t-shirt. I imagined that if I tried to fight him off, it would probably hurt me more than it would hurt him.

'Well?' he demanded.

I realised that I was still glued to the spot, staring up at him. His harsh voice woke me from my weakness and replaced it with a new bout of fear. I threw the chain at his feet, turned and ran. I ran as fast as I could carry myself. I ran straight past Hannah and didn't dare to stop and explain to her what had happened. Hannah, not much of a look-out, had been distracted by a passing boy and hadn't seen my encounter with the criminal, but she knew not to argue and followed.

We arrived at my house sweating and breathless. We proceeded to lock all the doors and windows before containing ourselves in my bedroom cupboard, a place we often hid when things went wrong. My mum knew not to bother asking. She never understood the importance of our missions. We sat cloaked in darkness on the floor of the cupboard, panting and coughing, waiting for air to reach our lungs again. Once I had caught my breath, I told Hannah about the man that she had missed and how scary he was. I described the chain I had found, which he surely would have used to tie me up had I not outrun him. We both decided there and then that this was a matter best left for the police, it was all getting too much. We ended our mission before we got ourselves killed, which we were convinced that we would. We never found out why the men were there or whether there actually was any criminal activity going on. But it never occurred to us that perhaps our imaginations had just run wild. I always waited for our next mission, but it never came. Hannah decided that games were for children and that she was 'so over it'. I began to worry if one day she would grow out of our friendship altogether.

It wasn't long after that, that Hannah showed her true colours for the first time. After she decided she was too old for games, her thoughts turned quickly to another life. A life that I never really understood but secretly dreamt of just as much as anyone else, (although I would never admit it out loud). A life of popularity and social acceptance.

In a way, Hannah was no different from any other girl in our class. She craved attention from the popular girls like a drug, and like any good drug addict, knew precisely how to hide her desperation when it suited, and expressed it like a true expert whenever it might work in her favour. Hannah spent most of her time and effort trying to get herself noticed enough to work herself into the inner circle of paper-thin popularity. In that respect, our school was no different from every other school in the world; controlled by that same familiar group that we all know and love, the popular girls, the 'in' crowd, the 'IT girls' – whatever you want to call them, ultimately, they are the same in every language. As you can imagine, any member of that group was unidentifiable as a single unit; they were all the same. The girls were blonde, slim, popular and the trendsetters for the rest of us. The type of girl that would never be caught dead without a guy on her arm and an adoring group of identical friends with identical personalities, hanging on their every word. The boys were equally as perfect. Anyone not part of their group was inferior to them and they were looked down on with disgust. That was their role, to be a higher power. They had their own territory in the schoolyard, their own section in the lunchroom that no one dared go near. They had an amazing power over every pupil in the school, I don't think anyone ever dared challenge it; no one had the guts to. But why try and change a system that apparently worked so well. It didn't work for me. I hated the system. Everything was so controlled. Why couldn't we do and say what we felt in our hearts?

Instead of sticking to what was thought of as socially acceptable. We weren't allowed to do certain things. We had to do other things. To defy the system would be social suicide. It's not that I purposely wanted to be different; I just didn't understand why it would be so terrible if I was.

Like every elite group, there was always one ringleader, who might as well have ruled the world. And no ringleader would be complete without a mindless circle of followers. Followers that spend most of their own time and energy holding on for dear life, clinging to a fickle popularity that could let go of them at any moment.

Jenny was the ringleader. She fit the role perfectly; pretty, popular and downright nasty. When she started to take an interest in Hannah, Hannah was overjoyed. She began spending more and more time with Jenny's circle and less and less time with her own. Eventually she was reluctant to even talk to me, her best friend in the world, who just couldn't give her what she needed - a platform, to spring into a new life.

A few weeks after Hannah started to hang out with Jenny and her circle, it was Hannah's birthday party. I had helped her plan it; it was fancy dress and we had chosen our costumes together. We were going to be a clown double act; we had a routine which we had practiced every day for weeks until we got it right. Everyone at school was going to be so impressed. When Hannah stopped talking to me, I assumed that I would no longer be welcome. So, imagine my surprise when the day before the party, my old friend Hannah came back to me. She insisted that we put the last few weeks behind us and that I had to still come to the party, and we would stick to our original plan, costumes, routine, the lot, best friends forever. I was so happy. It was over, everything would be ok.

The next day, I arrived at Hannah's house in full costume, big smiles and all. I was so excited to finally get my partner in crime back; I had missed her so much. I had spent the last few weeks wandering aimlessly, emotionless and full of defeat. Her mum let me in, letting me know that most of the other girls were already here. I practically bounced through to the backyard where I expected to be met by a sea of familiar faces.

Hannah shot up to greet me, 'Oh I'm so glad you came! Oh, and you wore a costume! How…nice.' She was wearing a hot pink tank top that showed off her belly button and a short denim skirt - not a clown costume.

'Where's your costume?' I asked.

She laughed maliciously in my face. '*Costumes,* are for children.' Disgust radiated through her voice.

My head turned to the other girls, not our other classmates as I'd expected, but Jenny and her circle. They stared at me with their mouths hanging open in shock for what felt like hours, before they doubled over into a fit of hysterical laughter. That was the moment I knew that my world had been crushed. Hannah had set me up on purpose, her initiation into her new club. My heart stung; humiliation coursed through my veins like a poison. My throat closed, unwilling to take in any more air that might force me to live through another moment.

I wish I could say that that was where the story ended, but really, that day was just one example of many in my friendship with Hannah. A friendship that I was always stupid enough and desperate enough to go running back to, every time she felt like it.

To me, friendship was, and still is, one of the most important pieces in the bigger picture, a picture of contentment. I value my friendships dearly and each one holds its own unique place in my heart. I would never dream of treating anyone the way I was treated by no other than my best friend in the world. As a child, I couldn't comprehend the idea of purposely causing another person pain. But even then, it was all around me. Nothing terribly heartbreaking ever happened during my childhood. I was not abused, I did not suffer any great loss, but these little things, they stay with you forever.

When I look back now at my childhood, I feel like I don't remember much of it. Either those years of my life were so numbingly uneventful that I have erased them from my mind, or perhaps I let the years of mind-altering abuse in my teenage years wash them away. Often, my mum or my brother will say, 'Hey, do you remember when we went here?' 'Do you remember when this happened?' And it makes me sad to say that no, I actually don't. But there are some memories that stay with you. Even if it might not make sense why your brain has chosen to remember your best friend's phone number from when you were five, but can't seem to consistently remember your log in password for your Hotmail account, which you use almost every day. Memories are funny that way. But surely there is method in the madness. Surely there is a reasoning behind what memories the brain decides to store, and what to throw away. It has not escaped me that the memories that my brain has chosen to store, the memories that are bright in my mind as if they were yesterday, both good and bad, are those in which I am pretending to be someone I'm not.

By the time I was ready to move on to high school, I was desperate to leave my childhood behind. High school was the first step towards adulthood, where the unreasonable need for children to be accepted by their peers, and the childish trauma of rejection would be left behind me, scattered into the dust. At least, that's what I remember thinking at the time.

I couldn't wait to meet all my soon-to-be new best friends and finally find a group that I could be part of unconditionally, just like everyone else seemed to have already found. I wouldn't have to worry about standing on the edge, overlooking other people's conversations. I would no longer be constantly waiting to feel that knife, slicing through the flesh on my back.

But high school, I thought. *High school will be different.*

Chapter 2 – Path to Popularity

When I was fourteen years old, I spent an entire summer grounded. To this day, it was the worst summer of my life. My friend Michelle and I decided to rebel and cut school for the day. We had skipped plenty of morning classes before; everybody did. As long as you check in at the school office before the lunch bell, you could usually get away with claiming you had slept in because your alarm didn't go off. They give you a late slip to take to your class and away you go, nothing else said. But cutting school completely, that was another story.

Excited about our first major rebellion, Michelle and I had already practiced forging our mums' signatures so that when we handed over our sick notes on our return to school, nobody would suspect that we had written them ourselves. There were only a few days left of term so we figured, even if they were a bit suspicious, they probably wouldn't bother to follow up anyway. We met in the morning just before the first bell and instead of heading to class, we got the bus into town instead. We spent the day high on life. This was by far the most exciting thing that either of us had ever done. Michelle had always been a goody-two-shoes, but just like any other good girl, she had a rebellious side just dying to get out and see the world. I, on the other hand, had always been up for just about anything, so it was really only a matter of time before we tried skipping out together. At the end of the school day, we headed back home just in time for the last bell, completely unaware that our parents knew exactly where we were and were patiently waiting for us when we got home.

As soon as I slammed the front door shut, I heard the line that every teenager dreads.

'Come in and shut the door.'

Hearing that is never good. And to make matters so much worse, it wasn't my mum shouting demands, it was my dad.

I was terrified of my dad, and I wasn't the only one. Our house was only a short walk from the school, and I would quite often invite friends home either to have lunch or on the way home from school. Usually, my dad would be at work. But when we got there, if my dad's car was in the driveway and he was home, more often than not, they would change their minds and decide not to come in after all. So the fact that he was the one bellowing to me to *come in and shut the door*, not to mention the fact that he was home in the middle of the day when he would normally have been at work, was worrying to say the least. The thunderous tone in his voice told me this is not the time for rebellion, so I did exactly as I was told. Door - shut.

'Sit down.' *Yes, sir.* 'Do you have anything you want to tell us?'

I swear I could hear him growling, his fiery breath building up in his throat, saving it up for whatever response I give him.

'No,' I answered, was there really any other answer?

He made several attempts here, but everyone knows that denial is key. He eventually started to lose patience, as he always does and I could feel the temperature in the room rising as his face turned beetroot red, as if it was bursting with rage. In the end, he exploded, letting his rage fly and I felt the force of his words pin me to the wall. I remember thinking, *'just stay quiet and let him finish, it will be over faster'*. Turns out, mine and Michelle's plan to cut school quietly under the radar had failed from the very beginning. Michelle had failed to mention that while we were skipping, she had missed a major test. Missing the test made her suspicious, which led to the school office calling Michelle's mum at home to inform her that her daughter was not in school. I could have absolutely killed her. Everybody knows never to try cutting when there's a test. When the school checked the register to see if any of her pals were off as well, they called my parents too.

My parents were horrified that I would do such an unruly thing as cutting class and grounded me for the whole summer. And although most parents say these things and then give in after a few days of moaning and pestering, mine meant it. I spent the entire summer behind bars, alone. It was probably the longest period of time that I had ever been on my own. And the problem with being on your own is that you only have your own insecurities for company. When left alone, there is no one to stop your thoughts from spinning out of control. By the time the summer was almost over, I was dreading going back to school. I had convinced myself that all my friends had long since forgotten me. After an entire summer forgetting what my face looked like, I wasn't sure they would still have a space for me. How would I ever fit back into a gap that had surely closed tight by now, without me being there to hold it open? After getting off to a bad start on the friendship front, I had little trust that any of my friends were really friends at all. And although I tried desperately to force myself to fit in with them, I always felt like I would never truly be one of them, maybe because I wasn't truly letting myself.

I had always been different. Always the one that no one ever took much notice of. And no matter how loud I would shout, sometimes I thought I must be invisible, that no one could hear me. At least, that's how it felt. I often wondered, if I faded away into my surroundings, without a word, would anyone notice? Was my presence ever of any importance to anyone other than me or would it go completely unseen, whether it was there or not. I always knew I was different from everyone else, tagging along behind, trying desperately to keep up with the majority, but never really sure whether or not I even wanted to. Always looking for that gap in the fence; the fence that kept me on the outside of the circle. A circle that part of me would have given my left arm to be included in, whilst the other part wanted nothing to do with it.

One night I dreamt that it was the first day back to school, only in my dream, I was excited. In the morning, I stood in front of my full-length mirror, holding up one outfit after another across my chest, before flinging it down onto the growing pile of discarded clothes mounting on top of my bed. I was so happy to be going back to school that I practically floated across my room to the wardrobe, where I continued to pull out more outfits. It had to be perfect, it had to make an impression, so that when I walked through the front doors everyone would think, 'WOW look at her, she looks amazing!'. I guess I thought it was the best sort of transformation I could hope for, that this year would be different.

After numerous outfit changes, I finally found the one. A black long sleeved *Kookai* top with the logo written across the chest in sparkling diamante letters, paired with obligatory uniform-appropriate black trousers that tightly hugged my hips and kicked out into flares at the calves, bang on trend. My hair had been flattened out with a straightening iron (something that doesn't happen easily or often), my makeup was subtle and sexy, making my eyes pop and hiding my flaws. I looked like a catalogue model. I struck several poses in my mirror before blowing a loving kiss to my reflection and strutting like a lioness out the door.

Once I got to school, I pushed open the double doors and breathed though the doorway, wind flying through my hair like a rockstar in a music video. Each person I passed turned their heads to gasp and marvel at my captivating beauty. A wave of admiration, as if the air around me glamoured them into my façade of elegance and beauty. The girls I passed by clung to me, gushing to tell me how great I looked, to ask where I'd been, how great it was to see me again. The boys stared in awe, desperate to be near me, under some whimsical spell where they fell to their knees at my feet. My long-term crush, Justin Thompson, collapsed in my path, breathing my name like a sonnet. I studied him for a second, judging his worth to be in my presence. I flicked my hair back irresistibly and snorted disapprovingly at him. I lifted my foot and pushed my sexy black patent platforms into his chest, pushing him back, where he faded back into my crowd of admirers. I watched Grease a lot that summer.

Suddenly, a massive gust of wind appeared. I braced myself, shielding my face from the wind. It lasted just a few seconds and I rushed to fix my superstar hair and get back to my adoring fans. I continued to strut my stuff, but this time nobody followed. As I walked, the crowd coming towards me, swarmed past me. One boy walked straight into me, banging into my shoulder, making me spin round and almost lose my balance. The shock of the collision had barely subsided when some else collided from the right, and then again from the left. As the crowd cleared and I found my footing again, I looked down at my hands. They were fading away in front of my eyes, I was disappearing. I started to panic, frantically shouting out to the people passing by me, but nobody could hear me. I grabbed for someone's arm but my hand sliced right through them like a ghost. I was invisible. I started to scream. Terrified, I started to run through the hallways, completely unseen and unheard. I woke with a jolt, sweating and breathless. Right back to square one.

In reality, my first day back to school wasn't quite as dramatic as how I imagined it. I didn't fade away into nothing, and my friends didn't forget who I was. But whether or not they noticed my absence at all over the summer was another question altogether. All I heard all day was *'Oh remember when we went here'*, and *'remember when that happened'*, *'It was so funny when that happened!'*. No, I do not remember when that happened. I wasn't there, remember? Now I was on the outside of a two month long inside joke; story of my fucking life.

Eventually summer faded into fall and I began to think things were going to be OK. I started hanging out with some new people, 'cool' people. I somehow managed to integrate myself into the 'Shop-mob', the inner circle which every teenage girl dreams of, an inner circle which I seemed to want and hate in equal measures.

The Shop-mob were composed of all the most popular people in each year, plus anyone who is accepted as being cool enough to be associated with them. It's a big club, but it's also pretty exclusive and hard to get into in. These girls have absolutely no worries at all. People on the outside were always talking about how horrible and fake they were, me included. And to some people, they were awful. But from the inside of the circle, things were different, they were actually…nice – or so I thought at the time. The embodiment of perfection - perfect hair, perfect skin, perfect figures, perfect lives. I would never in a million years have ever expected to be one of them. But all of a sudden, I seemed to have been accepted - as an associate at least. I hung out with them at breaks, ate with them at lunch. Elite by association, and that was good enough for me. Suddenly, I was starting to understand why so many people were so obsessed with popularity. Life was turning out to be pretty sweet. These kids ruled the fucking world, right from the very top of it. And who wouldn't want to be at the top of the world?

My complex on-off friendship with Hannah was very much back on again and we were BFFs once more. Hannah and I drifted apart when we first went to high school. We were put in separate classes with a whole bunch of fresh faces to get to know. But now in our third year, we had drifted back together. Hannah seemed to have grown up a lot since primary school and I easily forgot all the reasons why we drifted apart in the first place. But now, things were different. We were having so much fun together, it was like we were never apart.

Hannah was dating one of the hottest boys in our year, Justin, but she still always had time for me. Before long, two became three, and me, Hannah and Justin were practically inseparable. Justin, being the hottest boy in our year, was naturally part of the Shop-mob, making Hannah and I, Shop-mob by association. We began hanging out with them over weekends, where they introduced us to our new favourite past time - binge drinking. Luckily for us, and something that definitely seemed to work in our favour on the popularity front, Hannah's older brother Gary was old enough to buy us, and our new 'friends' booze.

Most Friday nights, Hannah would arrange to meet Gary outside the front of the shop, where the aptly named Shop-mob spent most of their time. The shop was a prime location for finding fellow shoppers that might be willing to buy alcohol for those of us who are not lucky enough to have older brothers. Fortunately, we didn't have that problem. Being seen at the local shop with Gary had several advantages:

1. He was an older boy (regardless of the fact he was Hannah's brother - he certainly wasn't *my* brother!)
2. He had hot older friends (friends who are not *Hannah's* brother!)
3. He had a car (enough said)
4. He could buy us booze (again, enough said)

Gary would pull up outside the shop in his kitted-out boy-racer style car, revving his engine to ensure he had everyone's undivided attention. The boys would *ohh* and *ahh* about how cool his car was, crowding around to check out the flash alloy wheels, the foot-high spoiler hanging off the back and the *epic* sound system which you could hear from halfway across town. The girls, less interested in the car and more interested in who was inside it, would hang back, playing it cool in front of any potential boyfriend material. Gary and his mates got the attention of everyone there and since it was us they wanted to see, we got their attention too. Gary would hang around and 'talk shop' with the other boys, while the girls would clamber over each other to get to us, desperate to be noticed by the boys with the cool car. It felt so strange to be the one that everyone wanted to talk to. Even if it was just to get closer to the cute boys.

After Gary had soaked up enough attention, he would go into the shop and get us the booze and fags that we requested. A ten deck of *L&B* and big fat bottle of *White Lightning,* a cheap cider with the appropriate nickname - *White Shite.* As he climbed back into the driver seat, he always did the same thing, his signature move. First, he'd turn to face the group of girls that were practically licking their lips at him. He'd flick his head back, just enough to see his eyes glistening from beneath his baseball cap. *'Later'* he'd say, no smile, no warmth, just pure coolness, before disappearing back into the driver seat and speeding off, like some sort of dark knight. Considering that I had known him when he was an annoying awkward twelve-year brat with acne and train-track braces, I found it quite amusing that he had somehow grown into this 'cool' guy, who everyone wanted a piece of. And although I'd never admit it to Hannah, I also found it quite sexy.

After he was gone, the girls would argue over who it was he spoke to. *'Oh my god did you hear that?', He wants to see me later!', 'No way, he was totally looking at me!', 'Don't be so stupid, why would he be looking at* you *when he could be looking at* me*?'*. It was like something out of an American high school chick-flick. In between flicking their hair back and pushing their chests out, I found it hilarious that this was *actually* how they spoke. Regardless, we were in a pathway to popularity. Pretty much the same thing happened every weekend and after a while, it was generally accepted that Hannah and I were part of the exclusive Shop-mob. I was so happy to be accepted by their group. But part of me never trusted it. Part of me always knew that it was only a matter of time before it all came crashing down around me.

One day, about half-way through the school year, I remembered why Hannah and I's friendship had broken down so my times. I was sitting in the playpark just outside the school grounds one lunchtime with my friend Ryan, when Sara Wilson, the queen bee of the Shop-mob girls, came storming over to us like a tidal wave. Sara was a nasty piece of work. Sara was the queen bee, not because she was blonde and pretty like most of the other girls, but because she was a bully, and nobody was brave enough to challenge her or her position. The most powerful weapon in the world – fear. Now that I had been accepted into the Shop-mob, the thought that she was coming to confront me never crossed my mind. Ryan had a bad habit of rubbing people up the wrong way, so I assumed he had done the same to Sara. But then she sailed straight past Ryan and came to stand facing me with a face like thunder.

'Have you been spreading shit about me?' she demanded.

Shit. My heart fell into my stomach. I had no idea what she was talking about, but these girls don't usually care about insignificant things like the truth. Once they find a reason to step on you, they hold onto it.

I tried my best to reassure her that I hadn't said anything about her and that I had no idea why she would think that. She continued to ask, saying she had heard from someone that I had been calling her a bitch and a whore. I frantically tried to convince her that I hadn't said anything of the sort, but it didn't seem to be getting through. My response was pitiful, I'm sure she must have been able to see me shaking, knowing that there was no way I could win this argument, and knowing what the potential consequences would be. Eventually, she seemed to accept that I wasn't going to give her the confession she was looking for and left me with a nice little warning, just in case I didn't quite get the situation. She warned me that if she heard again that I had been saying anything about her, then I was 'fuckin' dead'. *Naturally*, I thought. However, the most interesting part of the conversation came once she'd turned to walk away, and enough feeling had returned to my legs to take a few steps after her. I shouted after her, not quite sure what kind of reaction to expect, but I had to know.

'Will you at least tell me who told you that I was apparently spreading shit?'

She let out a cold, evil laugh as she shouted back to me, 'Hannah.'

The next day, once I had time to process yet another betrayal from my best friend in the world, I went to confront Hannah. She was the last person in the world I wanted to talk to. This was not the first time she had knifed me in the back like this. I at least deserved to know why. I had to ask her - how could she do this to one of the people who cares about her most in the entire world?

I saw her at the smoker's corner as soon as I came through the school gates in the morning, all over Justin like a rash. As I came towards her, she shouted to greet me, all sweetness and light like nothing had happened. I was stunned. I was so shocked by her complete lack of shame that, for a moment, I was speechless. Only for a moment. Once I found my voice again and the searing anger inside me reminded me why I was there, I yelled at her.

'What the fuck?! How can you act like nothing's happened?'

A pathetic 'deer caught in headlights' look came over her face as she looked to Justin for backup. She looked like she was going to cry. Hannah was always good at playing 'little miss perfect'.

I looked around at our other friends' faces, whose attentions held like stone. Hannah's doe-eyes crept their way around all the other confused faces and I could see I wasn't going to win this battle easily. I was so angry. All I wanted to do was rip her to pieces. I didn't even give her a chance to speak. By that point, I was no longer interested in anything she had to say. Hearing her fake excuses and letting her run her 'little miss perfect' act, wasn't going to change anything. Her doe-eyed innocent reaction was obviously enough to get the rest of the group on her side, so she didn't need to say anything. Other than denial, what could she really say anyway?

When I was done shouting, I turned away, gasping for breath. When my fury took over, I guess I forgot to breathe. The adrenaline surged though me like I was on fire. I could feel the rage pulsing through me like poison. I felt my gut rumble with fear, with excitement. I had never confronted anyone like that before. I'd always been too scared of being shot down or getting myself into more trouble. I'd always worried about what people would think of me. I had spent my entire life trying to be accepted by the people around me, the last thing I wanted to do was to make enemies. But that day, everything changed. I saw a different side to myself that day, a beast that had lay hidden all my life, being trampled into the dirt by careless passers-by. Like the incredible hulk, there was a beast inside me getting stronger and stronger. Now was the calm before the storm, but one day the storm would come, and it will destroy everything in its path.

For the rest of the week, I did my best to avoid pretty much everyone. I passed Sara a few times in the hallway, and although her scowls were threatening, she left me alone. After Hannah nearly turned me into the Incredible Hulk, I avoided her too. So far, I was doing a pretty good job of hiding away in the shadows and it seemed like things would do as they always do, and just blow over.

My rage, however, had not blown over. The monster inside me had not subsided and every time I had a moment of thought to myself, I was straight back there. Before long I was exhausted. Being angry all the time is exhausting.

That Friday night, I was attacked in the street. Sara had not forgotten, and neither had the rest of the Shop-mob. But it wasn't her that started it, it was Hannah.

I started off Friday night with some of my non-Shop-mob friends, Lauren and Sarah Dee. I had every intention of staying as far away from the shop as humanly possible. After the week's events, I wasn't exactly expecting a welcome committee from the Shop-mob, which now seemed to well and truly include Hannah. However, getting drunk is pretty difficult without anything to drink or anyone to buy it for you, so after a brief discussion about how much it would suck to hang about the shop, we went anyway, in order to find someone to buy us booze. We were pretty cautious to stay away from anyone too toxic, so we kept to the other side of the car park opposite the shop, away from the massive crowd accumulating outside of it. We hung back far enough so we wouldn't be seen by the Shop-mob but close enough that we could still catch a friendly looking passer-by, who might be willing to help us out with our alcohol dilemma. It didn't take long and eventually we were patiently waiting to find out if the stranger we had given all our money to, would indeed return with the cider we requested – thankfully, he did. After he handed over the carrier bag, I was anxious to get away from there. The crowd was growing quickly and any ridicule that Sara or Hannah wanted to throw at me would be in front of half the school. Now I think back, I would have gladly taken any name calling or threats they wanted to dish out, rather than what happened next.

As we turned to leave, I heard someone calling my name. I spun round to see Hannah storming towards me, closely followed by Justin and some other people. I ignored her and carried on walking. But she carried on shouting, calling me chicken for running away from her. I wasn't running from Hannah, I was walking. I had no reason to think that I might need to run. I tried to shout back to her that I wasn't interested in hearing her apologies, but she carried on charging towards me till she caught up with me. She had no intention of apologising. She started yelling and crying at me that I had no right to talk to her the way I did. I met her challenge of course and yelled back twice as loud. *Who the fuck did she think she was?!* As our shouting match grew louder, we started to draw a bigger and bigger crowd. As soon as Sara's name was mentioned in our argument, someone called her over. The angry rumble in my gut turned to fear, I knew then where this was going.

When Sara arrived, she pushed her way through the crowd to get to me, she didn't waste any time.

She started screaming into my face the same thing over and over, 'Are you shouting at Hannah? Are you fucking shouting at her?'

Obviously. But I knew that the better answer was to fall to her feet and beg forgiveness, arguing with her was not going to do me any favours. Then suddenly Becca, one of the other Shop-mob girls, pushed Sara out the way and took over. She was just waiting for an excuse to fight with someone, anyone, and the same went for Sara too. These girls needed to exert their authority every now and then, to remind anyone who was thinking of crossing them, what happens when you do. I was just the wrong person, in the wrong place, at the wrong time.

Before I knew what was happening, Becca started to hit me. Blows coming from left, right, left, right. And these girls don't bitch-slap like they do in high school movies, they punch, and they punch hard. Hard enough to make the world spin. Then somehow, I got away from her and managed to push my way through the crowd, working hard to put as much distance between us. By now, news of my impending demise had spread, and the crowd now consisted of everybody from the shop. There must have been at least fifty people, waiting to witness my humiliation at being outcast from the so-called elite. I broke through the crowd, guided by Lauren and Sarah Dee. I'm not sure how to explain what I was feeling. Lots of things, I guess. I was feeling that same rush of adrenaline I had before, but this time there was no anger, only fear. I was shocked, I had been totally blindsided and wasn't sure how it all happened. I was full of relief that it was over, it could have been so much worse. I'd seen this happen to plenty of other girls in our school and compared to some of them, I had gotten off lightly. She only managed to hit me a few times before I broke free. I felt no pain, a surreal numbness took over my body and the lack of feeling in my legs made it difficult to walk, I didn't get far.

Suddenly I was pushed hard from behind. In my brief, false sense of security, I was caught off guard. I wasn't able to catch myself and I fell to the ground. My head cracked hard onto the pavement and I was still for what felt like such a long time, but was probably only seconds. I wasn't sure if I was knocked out or just paralysed with fear. After a few seconds, everything else moved as the pavement spun around me. I managed to pull myself to my feet but as I tried to walk away, I stumbled blindly. My legs were not working, my head spun, and my vision dimmed. I didn't get much time to process anything before I was grabbed and pulled, and the punching started again. I was barely conscious, but I knew that this time it was not just Becca who was hitting me. I could feel punches and kicks from every direction, all throughout my body. I thought I was going to die, I thought that was it; *this is how my life will end.* The crowd roared and cheered, pleased to see what they came for, a public execution.

I was blind with fear, but somehow my body knew what to do even without my mind there to guide it. My survival instinct kicked in and I began punching whatever came in front of me with all the strength I had left. I had no idea who or what I was hitting, my vision was still gone. But it didn't matter, all I knew was that I was fighting back, I was fighting to survive. My *fight* or *flight* response. It felt like it was going on forever, but I still felt no pain. I could feel every strike that hit me, but they caused me no pain. I kept hitting. Adrenaline pushed me forward and I felt like I could keep going forever, aimlessly hitting out at the space in front of me in a blind frenzy.

Suddenly someone put their arms around me and held me still, someone stronger than me, bigger than me. I punched harder, thinking they were trying to stop me from fighting back. But as I hit back, he held me tighter, and I heard him whisper in my ear like an angel,

'Shh it's OK, it's OK, I've got you.'

As my vision started to clear and I looked up into the chest surrounding my head, relief captured me and pulled me closer to him. I recognised the *Adidas* logo of his sweatshirt; the sweatshirt he wore every day. It was AJ, one of the Shop-mob boys, one of the few good ones - he was holding me, and I was safe. I had never felt so much comfort in my life. As I surrendered myself to his embrace, I had no doubt in the world that he would keep me safe. I felt his body shift and I moved with him like we were one. I could still feel fists laying into my back, kicks up and down my legs, but my front was protected, and I knew it would be over soon. Suddenly he pushed me back away from him and I realised that he had broken through the crowds to the other side.

'GO!' he shouted as I stood, free, and for once, glad to be on the outside. AJ moved back through the crowd and I saw him holding Sara like a wild beast. Lauren and Sarah Dee were nowhere to be seen, no doubt still drowning in the sea of cheering spectators. I turned and ran. I ran like my life depended on it. I ran as if I could feel flames licking at my ankles. One wrong move, one missed step and I would be engulfed again in the fire. One wrong step, and I would be burnt alive. Again.

Over the weekend, I tried to process what had happened to me. But all my mind could do was spin and spiral. My mind, my body, my soul, everything, was completely overcome with betrayal, hurt and shame. The only thing that I was really sure of, was that nothing would ever be the same again.

I spent the weekend terrified about going back to school and what would surely be the second worst day of my life. Will they want to finish what they started? Will everyone be laughing at me? Everyone was there. Everyone in the entire school saw my shameful, public disgrace and execution. I was so humiliated. I almost wished it had been an execution, at least then I wouldn't have to go back to school and face them. At that moment in time, I would have gladly welcomed death. But maybe my execution was yet to come. Maybe this was only the beginning of the end.

Chapter 3 - The Beginning of the End

Monday came and went, and I was grateful to be allowed to stay home from school. I think my mum understood that I had a pretty genuine reason for not wanting to go. Unfortunately, it was only a one-day deal and despite pleading to never have to go back to school again, eventually I would have to face my fate.

"You'll have to face them sooner or later," she said.

Home schooling was not an option apparently. My mum tried hard to convince me that the best thing I could do was to go back and show them that I wasn't afraid of them. That they had no effect on me, and then they will leave me alone. She offered to go and talk to the school principal about the bullying, but truth is, I was never technically bullied. These girls had never shown any interest in me before, and neither had anyone else for that matter. I was just their entertainment for the night. Most likely by now, I would be long forgotten from their minds. I wish I could have said the same.

On Monday, Ryan came to the house after school to get the other side of the gossip he had been hearing about all day long. Ryan had been grounded over the weekend when he got caught stealing fags from his mum and so he missed out on Friday night's entertainment. He came knocking on my door as soon as school finished. He practically ran into the house, knocking me and the dog out of the way as he clambered inside the door, desperate to dish the dirt on what everyone at school was saying about me.

"OMG, I cannot believe I missed this! Tell – me - everything!" Ryan and I had been friends since primary school. But just like Hannah favoured popularity over her real friends, Ryan favoured drama.

"Nice to see you're so worried about me."

"Worried? Why would I be worried? You kicked all their asses! Everyone's talking about it! You're a fuckin' legend for putting those bitches in their places! If anyone should be worried, it's them!"

It seemed like the stories going around school didn't quite match up to how I remembered it. I wasn't being seen as the pathetic, hapless victim that I felt like; I was being seen as some sort of hero. He excitedly told me all the stories that were flying round school about what happened on Friday. I had to save a few nearby objects that were thrown from my dresser as they got caught in a crossfire of animated hand gestures that usually come with Ryan's 'drama queen' nature. He told me he spent most of the day trying to find out who all participated in my attack, for my benefit of course. Other than Becca, Sara and Hannah, two other girls, Sophie and Marie were also apparently part of it. Five of the Shop-mob girls in total. Five verses one.

This was the worst thing that had ever happened to me. Yet, people seemed be praising me. It seemed that, in my attempt to fight back against them, I did more damage on my own than they did as a group, to me. Ryan was impressed to see that I didn't have a scratch on me. I didn't mention to him that emotionally, I felt like I had been ripped apart at the seams and left for dead.

I did confess to Ryan that I was a bit scared of seeing the girls again, in case the same thing happened again, but he laughed. "You're kidding, right? Half the school is pissed at them and the other half is laughing at them. Trust me, they won't be coming anywhere near you again in hurry!" It was a comforting thought that I probably wouldn't have to worry about a second attack, but it didn't make me feel any better about the first.

When I returned to school the following day, I found that everything Ryan had said was true. From the moment I arrived till the moment I left, I was hounded, not just by my own friends, but by people who would normally never speak to me in a million years. Ryan was right, I was a legend. I'd never been so popular in my life. Overnight, I had earned a new respect and a *hard-ass* reputation. I wasn't convinced it was really deserving, but it was certainly amusing to see how differently people were acting around me now. The other girls in my year were suddenly hanging on my every word - telling me how much they love my top, skirt, pencil. I had to admit, it felt good having everyone looking up at me, instead of down, or even just looking at all. And if they wanted to see me as some sort of pseudo-hero for having my ass kicked by half the school's population of bitches, then who was I to stop them?

It's ironic that the most heartbreakingly painful, emotionally shattering and gut-wrenchingly shameful thing that has ever happened in my life, is the thing that finally put me where I always wanted to be - visible. I should have been glad that it was over. But it didn't feel over; it felt like it was only just beginning. I could feel myself changing. I could see my life changing in front of my eyes. Like someone turning down a dimmer switch. Everything around me was getting darker and darker.

With every day that passed, I could feel myself slipping away. I wished so hard for everyone just to leave me alone. I wanted to go to bed, put my head under the covers and never come out again. All that week, people went on and on about what happened. Every time someone mentioned it, I felt a sharp pain in my stomach, radiating throughout my whole body. And every time it happened, I felt I was moving further and further away from the world around me. I *wanted* to be further and further away. All I wanted to do was forget about everything. But I couldn't think of anything else but that night. Anytime I closed my eyes for more than a second, I would have flashbacks, diving me straight back into that night. Glimpses of panic, of fear. I felt their fists pounding into me, into my face and into my body, as if it was happening in real-time. Only this time, I could *feel* them. I could hear the crowds shouting and cheering. That's what made it worse, the crowd. The worst moment of my life made into some fucking spectacle for all to watch. Years to come people will say *"Oh remember when you had that fight at the shop? Man, that was fucking mental!"*. Yeah, I remember, how could I ever forget?

I was in so much pain all the time. Just the thought of being here, of being alive, made me feel panicked and hopeless. I dreaded every time I had to close my eyes for fear of being shot straight back to that night, the night when one world ended, and another began. The flashbacks were so strong, like pangs of terror radiating to my very core. Only I didn't see them, I *felt* them. The only vision I remembered clearly from that night was the stitched logo on AJ's *Adidas* sweatshirt, only now when I see it, it doesn't make me still like it should, like it did that night. Instead, it just brought more fear. And I heard the sounds. The crowds yelling, the fists pounding against my skin, my head cracking as I hit the ground. But mostly I remembered the fear, the wild panic that threw me back there, every time I closed my eyes. But when I opened them again, I was still here, still living and breathing, and the feeling was no better. I felt like I had lost who I was completely, everything felt different now. I could see myself in my mind, smiling and laughing. But now it is only a memory. Just like the feeling of smiling, of laughing. Memories.

Sometimes fear would turn into anger, and I felt like I couldn't control it. I felt it rupture in my stomach, like acid spilling out from my gut. Like it wanted to burst free and destroy everything in its path, extinguishing everything it touches. Sometimes I can't stop the rage from coming. Some days, by the time I got home from school, I was so angry that I would just scream. I wasn't able to stop it coming out. I felt it flow like liquid fire, spilling out from my chest. I was no longer in control of myself.

For the rest of that year, I felt like I was drifting silently away from reality, living in my own mind most of the time. It was easier there, on my own. All I wanted was to be left alone. I wanted to be as far away from the rest of the world as I could be. This society had broken me, just like I knew it had broken so many more before me too. I wanted no part of it; I didn't want to be associated with anything in it. I did everything I could to isolate myself, in the way I acted and even in the way I dressed. I stopped wearing colours, because I could no longer see them. I wore black, because it was the only colour now. I darkened my appearance as the world darkened around me, allowing me to hide in the shadows. At school, they called me a weirdo. They called me a Goth. But it was them who made me. It was because of them that I felt the need to change. To be as different from them as I could be, because I wanted no part of their world; the smiles and the laughter and the all the colours of the rainbow. They were all lies. There were no colours and no rainbows. There was only darkness. *I am the darkness.*

I found new pleasures in breaking things. The sound of glass or porcelain when it breaks, the way it shrieks in pain as hits the ground and shatters, excited me. I loved to see an object that once sat whole and undamaged, now in a million tiny pieces with no way of putting those pieces together again. Razor-sharp pieces, threating to cut anyone who tries to put them back together again. I broke things to stop me from wanting to break people. I wanted things to be broken in the same way that I was. I would pick up an object; the heavier the better, hold it over my head and scream as I smashed it down onto the ground in front of me. I felt a release of pressure in my heart when it shattered. My life was shattered. I had been thrown on the ground and broken into pieces. If I had to feel this pain, then so should something else.

I wanted the world to shatter. To end. To simply cease to exist. When the millennium came, the world cowered in fear that the world would be destroyed. Planes would fall from the sky and the world would ultimately come to an end. On Jan 1st 2000, when the world carried on turning as normal, I was disappointed.

Some days, I could feel the darkness lifting. Some days, I still felt like me. I couldn't understand it. I couldn't understand how some days could be so black and heartless and yet on others, I would feel the clouds shift, just enough to know there is still sun behind them. I was living my life from one day to the next, moving from one sunny day to the next whilst waiting silently for the storm to pass between them and for the sun to shine once more. I lived for sunny days.

I could feel my friends, the few I had left, giving up on me. And who could blame them? One day I am shiny and happy, and I am no different from them. Then the next, I can't stand to be around them. They didn't understand what was happening to me. How could they, when I didn't understand myself? Figuring it out is exhausting. On stormy days, I couldn't hear them talking to me because the screaming in my head was drowning everything else out. When I was in darkness, I wanted nothing more than to be alone, but being alone kept the darkness here longer. I was in darkness because I put myself there and I didn't have the strength to pull myself back out. On the days when the storms came, all my strength was used up, trying to stop it from pulling me down forever. Afterwards, there was no strength left.

Every day I forced myself out of bed and I forced myself to go to school, because it is easier than letting people see that I can't. I felt fear in my gut every time I thought about leaving the house. Ever since that night, I was so afraid to go out. The Shop-mob girls didn't bother with me at all afterwards, but then, they never bothered with me before that either, so it wasn't much comfort. There was still always the fear that they were just biding their time, waiting for me to forget, luring me into a false sense of security so they could meet me in some dark corner one night and finish what they started. Since being attacked, I stopped going out unless absolutely forced to. My friends were somewhat understanding about it, or at least they were at first. But now, after months of missing out, I was being left behind. At first, nobody pressured me to go out, then for a while they did, but then one day, they just stopped trying.

But just because the world seemed to be leaving me behind, it was by no means changing. The Shop-mob continued to terrorize the school one victim at a time. Later that year, once the worst night of my life had been long forgotten by the rest of the school, someone else's story was just beginning. Chloe was a few years younger than me and until the night that probably changed her life, just like it did mine, nobody even knew her name. I guess she was like me, an outsider that saw an opportunity to rise to the inner circle and ended up paying for her lack of judgement in humiliation and scars.

One weekend she was out at the shop, drinking cider with her new 'friends'. Chloe had too much to drink and passed out on a park bench. She was completely wrecked, unconscious, and they beat the shit out of her comatose body. She was completely defenceless against them, not even awake to try and fight back. It made me sick to my stomach to think that they have done this to someone completely defenceless, like Chloe was. I wondered if she knew what was happening to her or if she just woke up covered head to toe in dried blood and bruises with no recollection. She was lying passed out on a park bench when they pushed her off. She rolled off the bench into the mud, unmoving. The crowd that was gathered around her laughed. And if she had woken up and laughed it off then it might have been OK. But that's not what happened. She didn't wake up. She lay unconscious in the mud, surrounded by the same crowd that once surrounded me. Chloe lying there opened her up as an easy target and the Shop-mob girls started kicking her over and over, despite not so much as knowing her name. I thought about Chloe all weekend. Did she feel the same shame I did? Has she also lost what little faith she had in humanity around her after being beat to a pulp for literally being in the wrong place at the wrong time? But nobody needed to say anything. When she came back to school later that week it was written all over her face, painted in black and purple and yellow. She took a few days off school, but when she came back, she had a cut on her lip and on the top of her forehead. The bruising on her face had started to heal but was still plain to see. People talked about it for weeks, just the way they talked about me for weeks. When I thought about Chloe, I wondered if every time someone mentioned it to her, she wanted to scream at the world to stop turning, just like I did. I wanted so much to talk to her. To ask her if she was OK. To ask her, if that one night had ruined her life the same way it had mine. I wanted to know if she was able to move past it, like I should've been able to, but for some reason wasn't. But I couldn't. I couldn't talk to her. I couldn't talk to anyone.

For the rest of the school term, I counted down the days until the year was over. We were coming to the end of our fourth year and reaching the point in our lives where we were finally given the choice, whether to stay in school to do Scottish Higher exams, in preparation for university, or get out alive while you still can, with the bare minimum and go to college instead. Being one of the younger kids in my year, I would be forced to return after summer for half the year before I was old enough to enrol in college. But most of the Shop-mob would not be returning after summer. I thought that maybe once they were gone, I could try to find some sort of peace.

I would once again be able to walk to school every day, without being terrified that someone might be waiting, hiding just around the corner for me. I wouldn't have to be scared that I might bump into the wrong person in the school hallway or say the wrong thing in English class and that it will start all over again. They had long forgotten me and what they did to me on the night I first gave up on the world, but no matter how hard I tried, I hadn't forgot. I thought about it every day. Every time I heard footsteps behind me, I remembered being hit from behind when my defences were down. I heard footsteps behind me and my heart raced. My palms sweating, I would quicken my own steps, trying to put more space between me and the pending danger behind me. So many times, when I would hear someone, anyone walking behind me, I would panic and run all the way home. There were certain routes that I simply wouldn't take. Long pathways where there were no side paths to form escape routes. Paths where if someone started walking towards me, there would be nowhere to go except forward or back.

But next year things would be different. Next year I wouldn't be in fear. They would be gone, and everything would be different. A lot of my own friends would also be leaving, and I would be mostly alone. Depending on whether I was having a good day or a bad day, changed whether I thought this was a good thing or a bad thing. On my good days, I didn't want them to leave. I didn't want to be left here on my own. But on bad days, I looked forward to them leaving, almost as much as I waited for the Shop-mob to leave. On bad days, I couldn't wait to be on my own.

As a means of release, I began to write. I kept journals. I wrote short stories. Poems and song lyrics that would probably never be put to any music. Anything that wanted out, I let it out. Spilling out my deepest thoughts and fears to the only thing that would listen. I couldn't talk to any of my friends or family, so I talked to the blank and judgeless pages of my notebook. Sometimes writing helped, but sometimes it just makes things worse. When I felt angry or desperate, I would write, but during the good days, the words wouldn't come the same way. But on bad days, I didn't have to find the words, they would find me. The emotions ran so easily from my heart to my pen without ever touching my lips. It was this missing step that let them breathe so effortlessly; not having to say the words out loud. They were uncensored. They were true. On the days that hurt the most, I could write song after song without ever coming up for air. I let my anger flood the pages like a tsunami, awash with betrayal and grief at the loss of a world that never truly existed in the first place. Despair, that's all that was left. When you pull the covers away to reveal that what is underneath, is rotten. Words run page after page like a river. A river that has burst its banks after years of holding back the rushing water. A riverbank that no longer has the strength to stand on its own. On days when things were clearer, I would look back over the words that had been spilt during the days I spent in darkness, with no recollection of the words that had been written. Words that could easily have been written by somebody else, the only evidence being that it was my handwriting that formed them. When I let my emotions flow, it consumed me, and there was nothing else.

Some days, I painted. On good days, when I was able. It felt so good to do something productive, something that I could look back at and remember the good times. They were so few that when they came, I needed to savour every moment. So, I would paint something I could see every day, so that every day I was reminded that just behind all those thick grey clouds, there was sunshine. I used my bedroom walls as a canvas and painted colourful murals to inspire myself to carry on, at least until the next sunny day. They were never really paintings of anything in particular, sometimes just spirals of colours and flowing shapes. But it's not always about the subject of the painting; it's about *why* the painting needed to be painted in the first place. It's about the story it's trying to tell. My paintings reminded me that there are still days where I *wanted* to paint. They reminded me that there are still days where I was capable of creating something bright and beautiful. But mostly, they reminded me that there are colours. There are so many colours. My life had become so dark. My hair and my wardrobe and makeup, styled to match the darkness inside me, was almost entirely black. Yet somewhere inside me, I knew there was still yellow and pink and red and blue and green. Sometimes I just needed a reminder of that.

Where my artwork brought me comfort on good days, music brought me comfort on the bad ones, and still does. Like any other teenager, my musical choices changed dramatically over the years. Like every pre-teen girl, I began with the usual obsessions with pop stars. Unreachable, commercially manufactured pop bands, whose main purpose is to provide popular culture floor fillers and often inappropriate role models and heart throbs for young girls to idolise. However, as I grew older and wiser and developed my own sense of opinion, I came to realise that music's sole purpose is not to provide a backing track for teenage karaoke parties or to allow us to learn patronising dance routines, the purpose of music is expression. It is a story to be told, emotions to be heard and felt. It is a chance to see the world through the eyes of another. It is an art form and the means of expression. Once you understand that music is about the message, not the messenger, you are forced to re-evaluate something that is often a huge part of people lives. When I was a pop fan,

I never considered music to play any role in my life. Stranded on a dessert island in silence, I doubt I would have ever even noticed my loss. Now, stranded on a desert island with no music, I have no doubt that I would die of starvation, from a lack of human connection. The music I grew into, and the music I still listen to today, is real. It is not sugar coated that every love story will have a happy ending. Nobody proclaims that friendships can stand the test of time and will last forever and ever. Nobody pretends that the biggest issues that any of us will ever have to face, is whether or not the cute boy will ever notice me and whether or not he will love me forever.

When you step outside of your own bubble, when you try to see the world from someone else's eyes, you will see that there are much bigger issues out there and much more important stories to be told and heard. This world is full of pain and hate and malice. While we wallow in self-pity over our most recent break up, there are people dying of poverty and starvation. There are whole villages torched to the ground in religious and political protest. There are people hurting, dying, needlessly all over the world. People deafen themselves to these truths, preferring to hear about broken hearts and how much our pop stars love to party all night. The fact that our society can wholeheartedly pretend that real problems didn't exist, only gave me even more reason to want to distance myself from the world. I found a connection with music that is real. It is written by real people, with real problems, real opinions and real stories to be told. Sometimes, it is harsh and rash and so full of anger, hatred and despair, just like I was, and sometimes even still am now. Just like we all are sometimes.

The music didn't always make me feel like there was light at the end of the tunnel, but it did show me that maybe I wasn't the only one in the tunnel. Sometimes I could relate so strongly to the lyrics and I could feel the emotion of the music, not just the lyrics, but the guitars and the drums and the bass. I felt it rivet right through me like it's telling me that it *knows*, and that it's right there beside me. At the times I needed it, I felt closer to some of those songs than I did to any human beings. I felt so much comfort knowing that I'm not the only one in darkness. It gave me hope that maybe someday I would find someone else in this place. We would find each other, in the dark of the tunnel and we would save one another. The anger and hatred I heard in the music, gave me hope that there was someone else out there, lost in the darkness, just like I was.

Chapter 4 – Summer Lovin'

I was thankful that when the last day of term came around, I was on a good day and the world didn't seem so bad. And I even met a boy. A boy who seemed to have appeared out of nowhere and made the whole world worth it, in just a single day.

The last day of term is not your typical school day and generally involves drinking whatever you can find in your parents' alcohol cabinet, smoking weed in the park and either not going to classes at all or going to class *after* smoking in the park. That morning, Ryan picked me up to walk me to school just as he did every day. When we got to school, we waited just outside the school gate. Everyone knew this was the meeting point for anyone who felt like cutting class and was looking for someone to cut with. On the last day of term, there was never any shortage of people waiting at the front gates. Shop-mob territory was at the back of the school. Schoolyards are all about territory. By the time the final morning bell sounded at 8:45 a.m., there were 12 of us heading to the park, where we planned to spend the morning.

As soon as we all settled in at the playpark, the booze started to flow. Those of us who were savvy enough to be able to somehow procure our own booze, came armed with litre bottles of cheap vodka and huge bulging bottles of *White Lightning* cider. Those of us not lucky enough to look over 18, or who didn't have older siblings to buy booze for them, raided our parents' alcohol cabinets at home. Coke bottles filled with a dirty mix of vodka, rum, whiskey, sherry, just a few shots worth of each so not to drain the bottles so much they would be noticed. Either way, booze was booze. A dirty pint was still a pint, and it was good enough for us. By the time the lunch bell went at 12:15 p.m., more than half the booze had been drank and a few soldiers had already fallen. Those still standing headed back to school for lunch, ravenous from our morning of drinking.

The last day of term was a marathon, and nobody wanted to have the shame of not being able to last the day. A few had already thrown up their breakfasts in the park that morning, and after the greasy canteen food hit our stomachs, we lost a couple more. But there would always be more people waiting by the front gates at the end of lunch, planning to cut class for the afternoon.

During lunch we hung out at school. We ordered as much food as our lunch money would allow in an attempt to soak up some of the alcohol and make way for more, and caught up with some other classmates who had missed out on the morning anecdotes. Our school was centred around a large glass roof atrium, where corridors of classrooms run off to either side. It was a huge open space filled with plants, trees and lots of benches and picnic tables where students could hang out during breaks. During those breaks, it was crammed so full of students that you would be very lucky to ever find a bench. But we had a bench. We had *'The Bench'*, our own territory within the school where all of the *outcasts* congregated. Nicely situated between the science and art corridors, and close enough to the canteen, that we didn't have to navigate through seas of people from the other end of the atrium just to get food. At school, I hated to be alone. But I always knew that if I went to The Bench, I was highly likely to find someone that I knew remotely enough to pass 10 minutes with until the next bell sounded, and we all piled into our classrooms. It was at The

Bench where I met the boy that would become my first love, Jamie. I was talking to a fellow *Bench* regular, Stevie, about who was coming back to school after summer and who would be leaving. Now that we had done our Standard Grade exams, school was no longer mandatory and many of us would be leaving. Since my 16th birthday wouldn't be until October, after the school term had started back after summer, I wasn't able to leave until Christmas. So, I would be returning after summer whether I wanted to or not. Jamie casually inserted himself into our conversation. Before he had a chance to contribute anything to our conversation, the bell rang. People streamed around us in all directions. As we stood amongst them, it reminded me of the still centre of a storm, like we were untouchable.

"Are you going to be here next year?" he said, only to me.

His huge brown eyes caught mine, holding them there like a hypnotist, waiting for my answer and taking my breath away at the same time.

"Yeah, I'll be here," I gushed.

I was taken aback by this gorgeous guy wanting to know my whereabouts.

His flawless olive skin looked like it would taste of sweet caramel. I wanted to taste him. His big brown eyes were dark like black holes, ready to swallow me whole.

"Good," he said.

He held my gaze firmly and I saw a sparkle in his eyes that made my stomach flip.

In that moment, all I could think about was how much I wanted him to grab me and pull me into him and kiss me; a scene that re-ran in my mind constantly through the rest of the day. He turned away, ready to merge back into the crowds of people moving to their next classes, but then he stopped and turned back to me.

"I'm Jamie, by the way," he said smiling, before vanishing into the masses as if I had imagined the whole thing.

I just stood there for the longest time, not sure how to handle the sudden attention. I knew from that moment that I would spend the entire summer waiting to see that smile again. Suddenly, six weeks went from being not long enough, to an eternity.

When I finally managed to float back down to earth, Ryan was standing in front of me, cross-armed and grinning from ear to ear. After witnessing Jamie and I's encounter, he then spent the rest of the afternoon singing "Gill and Jamie sitting in a tree K-I-S-S-I-N-G", the rest of the crowd also merrily joining in my ridicule at the most public crush I've ever had. By the end of the day, I was glad to get to go home and hide in my room, alone, and wait for my embarrassment to die down.

Summer began in the usual uneventful way. No school, no books, no getting up at stupid o'clock everyday – it's like every day is a Saturday. And after so many months of longing, desperate to be left alone, I was finally getting it. I was alone. Other than my own family, I hadn't seen another person in over a week. Just what I always wanted. That was, until one day when I got a surprise visitor at the front door, which turned everything upside down.

I was happy wallowing in my own self-pity. Generally enjoying not having to put on any kind of 'show', enough to enable me to be around other people; and I had absolutely no intention of endangering that by trying to venture into the outside world or interacting with other people.

When the doorbell went, I ignored it. Why wouldn't I, it's not like I get many random visitors in the middle of the day. My mum came into my room with a massive smirking grin, my brother giggling from behind her.

"You've got visitors!" she practically sang at me.

"Who?" I demanded.

Who could possibly have gone to the bother to come visit me? As well as being fairly confused, I was also quite annoyed. I was quite happy hiding in my room away from the rest of the world and didn't need to be disturbed. I was also quite conscious that I looked hideous. I looked down at what I was wearing, mortified at the idea of someone seeing me like this. Adidas bottoms that went out of fashion years ago, splattered with paint and hair dye, an overgrown hoodie two sizes too big, which didn't match my bottoms, and I hadn't washed my hair in several days. I was a mess. I may be wallowing in self-pity, but I was still a fifteen-year-old girl with a reputation to uphold.

"You'll just have to go and see, won't you?"

I heard Dylan giggling like a little girl, and I had to force myself to swallow my desire to punch him in his annoying little face. I settled for a swift kick in the shin as I pushed past him, plunging myself back into my room to change my hideous clothes.

"Ahh, Mum, she kicked me!" he whined as he bent over in pain – crocodile tears as always.

I ignored him as I tore off my old clothes and slid quickly into something more presentable, before even knowing who was at the door. For once, my mum also let it slide and ignored him – there were more exciting things afoot.

Now in more acceptable attire, I nervously, slowly pulled the door open, heart literally in my throat, only to be met by two somewhat drunken boys whaling out *'Wonderwall'* at the top of their lungs. Future boyfriend Jamie, the boy I had spent the last week dreaming about, imagining that he probably didn't even remember meeting me, along with Stevie, were serenading me on my doorstep. I stood stunned. If I had been a cartoon, my jaw would have hit the floor - whether in shock, or shame. I heard Dylan erupt in laughter, but it was easy to ignore with the racket coming from the driveway. I didn't know whether to cry or laugh. One thing I did know – my mum and my brother were never going to let me live this down. I stepped outside to try and stop the embarrassment from seeping into the house. I looked back at Dylan and my mum as I closed the door behind me, sniggering away together like schoolgirls who'd caught two of their teachers kissing in the supply closet.

They continued to sing the entire song and I could feel my cheeks getting redder and redder. I looked around at the neighbours' houses to spot any curtain twitchers – thankfully, it didn't seem like anyone had noticed them. When they got to the end of the last verse, caught in the momentum, they carried on into a round and began singing the song again from the beginning, *'Today is gonna be the day…'*. And when they clung to each other and took off in a waltz around the driveway, I got the feeling I had been forgotten about. After the initial shock passed, all I could do was laugh. It was either laugh, or cry.

When they finally ran out of steam, I managed to get out of them that Stevie's parents had left him alone for the weekend and they had decided to celebrate by spending the day raiding his dad's drink cabinet – dirty pints, no doubt. They rambled on drunkenly for a while about their antics that day, whilst constantly interrupting themselves to ask, 'Did you like the song?', 'But you liked the song, didn't you?', 'Of course, you were both very good!' I told each of them every time they asked. At the start of that day, I didn't know Stevie or Jamie very well. But by now, I had fallen in love with both of them. Although, definitely one more so than the other!

Suddenly, Stevie moved his face closer to mine and pressed his finger against his lips.

'Shh', he said, swaying back and forth, his eyes going together slightly. 'Do you want to know a secret?' he asked, serious face on.

'Always,' I smiled, indulging him.

'We got drunk on purpose!' He burst out giggling.

'Well yeah, that's usually the point,' I responded, just thinking he was being, well, drunk.

'So that Jamie could ask you out!' he blurted out, practically rolling about on the ground laughing.

My heart started somersaulting from my chest, into my stomach, up into my throat, and back to my chest again. I guess he heard about the whole "K-I-S-S-I-N-G" charade on the last day of term. Was he mocking me? I was so nervous, I couldn't even speak. Jamie, who up until this point had not been paying attention and had instead been checking out the wheel trims on my mum's Cavalier, was suddenly back with us. They argued drunkenly back and forth as Jamie protested that he was 'talking shit'. And when the arguing turned into a play wresting match in my driveway, I left them to it. Again, I got the distinct impression that I had been forgotten about. They reminded me of the puppet show that we used to watch in the park as kids - Punch and Judy – *'Oh no he didn't! Oh yes he did!'* After indulging them for 20 minutes or so, I didn't really feel my presence was making much of a difference, so I kindly advised them that perhaps they should go home and sober up, and that they could apologise for the sheer embarrassment that they had caused me when I next saw them. After some persuasion, they finally left. I closed the door and stood with my back against it, waiting for the blood in my veins to resume normal flow. I was beaming uncontrollably from ear to ear. Suddenly, there was another knock at the door. This time, it was just Jamie. I felt my heart beat harder and faster and blood raced through my body.

"Em, hello, again," he said sheepishly.

His mischievousness had been replaced with a vulnerability and nervousness which made me melt.

"Hello, again!" I replied, trying to act suspicious of why he had come back again, alone, but secretly wanting to run out the door and kiss him.

"Err yeah, sorry about that. Stevie can be such a dick."

"I agree."

I couldn't hide my smile anymore. He made me feel like a lovesick puppy, and the butterflies in my stomach really were making me feel sick.

"Yeah. So, em, I'm gonna be down south all summer at my gran's, so I won't be around. But I was hoping maybe I could, like, call you, or something, over the holiday? Or you could call me? You know, just if you want to?"

I could practically see the sweat dripping from his brow. My heart was beating so loudly, I couldn't hear myself think, and the butterflies were ricocheting so hard off my insides, I thought they might break free. I tried to think of something clever and sarcastic to say to him, but one look in his eyes and I melted once again.

"I guess that'd be OK," I shrugged. *Cool as a cucumber.*

"Cool," he said, unable to hide his relief.

For a minute we just stood, coy and awkward, not sure what else to say to each other and smiling shyly whenever our eyes met.

"Jamie, have you done it yet? Hurry up or I'll leave without you!" Stevie shouted from behind the wall.

We both laughed, relieved that he broke our awkward silence.

Stevie's face cautiously slid round the side of wall, "Psst, are you done yet?" somewhere between a shout and a whisper.

"Em...," Jamie's nervous laugh gave it away.

"Guess so. Come on then, let's go!" Stevie shouted impatiently.

"I eh, I guess I better go," Jamie said shyly.

"But em, I'll speak to you soon, yeah?" he held out his hand to me.

My fingers brushed against his as I took the piece of card in his hand. As we touched, sparks of electricity shot through my body. I felt my heart rate double.

"Guess so." *Cooler than a freakin' cucumber.*

"OK then, see you soon."

He started backing away, reluctant to leave.

"Speak to you soon," I said smugly.

"Bye then."

He barely noticed as he walked backwards into the wall. I couldn't stop myself from laughing at him.

"Oh," he said, turning around to see what had stopped him. "Sorry, didn't see you there," he said to the wall.

When he turned back to me, he seemed a bit more relaxed, pleased that he had made me laugh. Stevie suddenly reappeared from behind the wall and raised his hand cheerfully to salute me.

"Bye!"

He threw a massive cheesy grin my way, grabbed Jamie by the arm, and yanked him out of view. It was like something out of a Carry-On film. Just at that, Stevie's head reappeared from behind the wall.

"He really likes you, you know," he nodded knowingly, and then disappeared.

My heart sang. For the first time in I don't know how long, I heard the birds sing in the trees. I looked down at the card in my hand. It was about the size of a business card and the edges around the outside were decorated with tiny daisies and bumble bees buzzing between the flowers. Handwritten on the card were the lyrics to Wonderwall. Reading them made my heart melt.

We hadn't had a full conversation together yet, but somehow, already, we had our own song. I wondered if he thought about me when he listened to it. I turned the card over in my hands, expecting to find Jamie's phone number on the other side, but instead he had written his email address. My heart sunk. *What the hell am I supposed to do with this?* He said he wanted to chat – how can we *chat,* if he doesn't give me his number? I wasn't even sure how I was going to email him. We had a PC, but its sole purpose was *Roller-coaster Tycoon,* and I was pretty sure that there was no email function. Panic sunk in as I realised that I had to somehow figure out the wizardry of email, otherwise, I wouldn't get to talk to Jamie again for another six weeks.

This new predicament took pride of place over my embarrassment and I immediately sought counsel with my mum and brother. Thankfully, they were both so excited at the idea of learning how to send an email, that they overlooked the fact that Jamie had practically asked me out. Together, we managed to conclude that our computer wouldn't send emails because it didn't have dial up and isn't connected to the internet. Luckily, and thanks to our family brainstorming session, we realised that we should be able to send an email through the TV, through the *Sky Interactive* function; Which I didn't quite understand, but my 11-year-old brother, who probably couldn't even spell interactive, seemed to know exactly how to use.

In order to remain *cool as a cucumber*, I waited the obligatory two days before calling (or in this case emailing) Jamie – so not to come off too desperate. Two days after my doorstep serenade, me, Dylan and Mum all gathered excitedly around the TV to send our first ever email together, as a family. Although, admittedly, it did seem a little strange that it would be to a boy I fancied from school. I had spent the last two days trying to decide what to write. If I got it wrong, he may not write back – so it had to be perfect. Still playing it cool, I decide to avoid the obvious choice of *'OMG I'm so glad you asked me out! I think you're so cute! Say that you'll love me forever!'*. I felt that was perhaps a bit much (especially considering that my mum and brother were helping me write it). Instead, I decided to go for simple, short and sweet - *'So nice to see you the other day. Hope ur havin' a good holiday...here's my number* (in order to try an avoid an emailed response which I may never figure out how to find!) *hope to hear from you soon...'*.

After about half an hour or so, we finally found the option to send an email. I started to hope more than ever that *if* Jamie ever received my email, he would decide to reply by text, since I wasn't convinced that I would ever be able to find the email option again. After quite a while of losing myself in various menus and options, I finally found the option to send an email and I was ready for my first draft. My message took about 20 minutes to type in via the remote control, where I navigated through an onscreen keyboard using the directional buttons, something that was completely new to all of us. By the time I was done typing, Mum was itching for a tea break. Email typed, kettle boiled, now just to hit send and it's done. But when I hit send, nothing happened. I hit it again. The screen glitched and my email disappeared. Did it send? Did it delete? How do you know if the email sends or not? I expected some sort of receipt, but I never got one. So just to be sure, I retyped the whole thing and sent it again. Then I tried again, and again, and each time it kicked me out, and it was gone. I grew more and more frustrated, and each time I had to retype it, the message got shorter and shorter. What had started as about six lines of text, ended up as *'please call me on 07975313201, Gill x.'* I left it at that – no idea whether or not my email had actually gone anywhere and if anyone would ever receive it.

By the end of the afternoon, I no longer ever expected to hear from Jamie again. I started the day full of excitement and hope at the idea of starting my new summer romance. But by the end of the day, I had fallen back into my pit of self-despair, convinced that he would surely forget about me over summer anyway, if he hadn't done already.

Story of my fucking life.

Chapter 5 - Darkness and Light

One day, everything went black. Not for any particular reason – it just did.

I could feel the darkness creeping. I felt it seeping into my veins and pulsating through the chambers of my heart, blackening the muscles like a poison. I felt it wrapping its shadowy fingers around my soul, squeezing out any remnants of sunshine. My poisoned muscles were weak, and I couldn't fight it anymore. My body was overcome and blackened, like a chameleon against the black world surrounding me. I had been waiting for this day, and now it was here. I watched silently as everyday my world grew colder. From an ever-cold grey mist, to twilight, and now finally to an eternal darkness. I thought I would miss the sun more. Even through the mist, I knew it would clear, if only for a day. That one day was always enough to remind me that underneath it all, out there somewhere, far through the mist, the sun would shine bright and the sky would be blue and clear and full of hope. I thought I would miss it more. But when the clear sky vanished and the sun stopped shining, I could see the truth. I had been blinded by false hope. I had been shielded from the truth of what this world really was, what it was meant to be. Now that the hope was gone, I could accept my place in this new, dark world.

When the light faded, so did my ability to release from the pain I was in. My mind withered and dried and there was no art, no song that could ever be strong enough to pull me out from under this. I was bound and chained, and I could do nothing but lie there and feel it. It was all I deserved. I created this new world and the pain and hopelessness it brings was mine to suffer. This was my punishment for being weak. My sentence, for not being strong enough to fight back.

One night, whilst the world around me was in darkness, I found a new release. A way to take away the dark, just for a second. Just for a second, I found a way to replace the pain I was feeling with something else, another type of pain. But this was a pain that I at least understood. I took a knife, pushed the blade hard against my skin and I cut myself. Even now, I can't explain why I did it or even where the notion to do something so disgustingly awful came from, only that somehow, it did. It is something terrible, and it is something beautiful and I can't explain it. Maybe it was because it was a type of pain which I could control, something I could understand. Or maybe it was about converting one type of pain into another. Like how energy can't be destroyed or displaced, it can only be converted into another form of energy. Afterwards, I couldn't believe I could do this to myself. To think about the knife cutting across my flesh made me sick to my stomach. I was disgusted at myself, that I could turn to something so terrible. My mind was already destroyed and now I had turned to destroying my own body. The first cut was deep, and the scar will stay with me for a long time, but the mental scarring will stay with me forever.

When the blood that dripped from my skin had dried, all that was left was shame. But when the blood ran red and fresh and clean, I felt a weight lift from my shoulders, shoulders that carried a world of pressure, crushing the bones that bore the weight beneath it. I was sickened at myself for this terrible, horrible thing. Yet, it was the most free I had felt in so long. It was almost as if the pain that was constantly circling my veins was released through the cut, pouring out of me along with the blood. I knew even from the first time, even through the shame and disgust, that it wouldn't be the only time. It would happen again, and again. It will call to me, just like it did that first night, and I will cut, again and again. I couldn't explain it, yet, why should I have to? It was my life and my body. If this is the thing that will allow me to have any sense of relief, then so be it. When everything else has gone to shit, why shouldn't my own flesh?

Eventually my scars healed, but the memories of that hideous act will stay with me forever. I continued to be disgusted at myself for letting things go so far. I hated myself for letting this happen. How could I let this happen? How could I let this go so far that I had resorted to mutilating my own body? I had put myself here. I had cut myself out of my own life, just like I tried to cut the pain from my skin. I pushed myself away from my friends, from my own family. But when the whole world went into darkness, I knew there was no way to fix it. Even if I had let someone try, I couldn't be saved.

*

My mother is the kindest person you will ever meet. And when she smiles, really smiles, there is a sparkle in her eyes that sings like a sweet lullaby.

When I was a little girl, whenever I had a scratch or a bruised knee, I thought her touch had magical healing powers. When I was around five or six, I remember running home to my mum like my life depended on it;

certain that if I didn't reach her in time, I would simply drop dead on the spot. I had gone out to play one day and after knocking on the doors of every other child in our street, and failing to find a playmate, I went out to play alone, possibly for the first time in my life. I decided to head to the local park for the afternoon. Which, thinking back, was probably quite far for me to be venturing alone at that age, but then, perhaps that's the reason I went. I imagine that my mum was not aware of this at the time.

I went to one of the spots frequented by my friends and I on our way home from school, a small clearing in a patch of wildland where a thick fallen tree trunk made for a perfect '*house*', where we would play the aptly named make-believe game of '*house*'. As I played in the brush alone, sweeping the dirt ground with a broken tree branch and organising the twigs scattered on the ground into a neat and tidy pile ready for a make-believe fire, something prinked my finger. At first, I didn't think much of it. But after a few minutes, when I saw the bright red smear dripping down my makeshift sweeping brush, I looked down at my hand to find it streaked with blood. I remember standing stunned, staring at the blood, watching the drops, thick and heavy, falling to my newly swept floor. It was the first time I had ever seen my own blood. In the centre of the red patch on my thumb, sticking out sharp and black, was a thorn. It took a few moments for the panic to set in. The first thought in my head: *"Mum!"* I dropped everything and ran. I ran like I had never run before. I ran as if I were being chased by a pack of ravenous wild dogs, hungry for a taste of the blood pouring from my thumb. I screamed past people walking their dogs, other children out playing. Tears stung my eyes as the wind on my face pushed them inwards, stopping them from falling but rather remaining in my eyes, saving up all the pain I was suffering until I could reach the only person in the world that at that moment, even existed. When I was about halfway home, I ran straight into the arms of Gregor, a teenage boy who lived on our street. I didn't even see him as I ran, but as I ran towards him, he cast his arms wide and caught me in them as I flew past him. He cried at me with such concern that he was almost as upset as I was. He held me still, demanding to know what was wrong and how he could help me. Unfortunately, I was quite scared of this boy. I couldn't tell you why now, but I must have had my reasons at the time. So, the boy only made me worse. I remember screaming at him, *"There's a thorn in my thumb! There's a thorn in my thumb!"* A tongue-twister under normal circumstances, but imagine you are six, have half your teeth missing and are crying so hard that your hair has matted against your face as if there had been a monsoon. Gregor tried several times to understand what I was saying, eventually giving up and releasing his grip on me. I bounded away from him like I was elasticated and didn't stop until I was in the loving arms of my mum. I didn't have to explain to her what was wrong. I hid my face in her chest and cried until she told me it was over. When I looked back at my thumb, the thorn and the blood were gone. She took my still throbbing hand between hers and lifted it to her lips. She kissed gently where the thorn had been. The thorn that caused me so much pain that I thought I was dying, and just like that, it was all gone. She looked up, smiling at me "There you go. I kissed it all better."

*

Every now and then, I would feel the clouds lift and the sun shine in. I came to cherish those days, the days when there was sun, and colour, and love and light. I missed them when they were gone. But remembering the good days, no matter how insignificant they may seem to anyone else, got me through the days when the sun never came.

Every summer, Dylan and I were dragged around every garden centre within a twenty-mile radius, on the promise of an ice-cream on the way home. We follow patiently while mum *"ohh"ed* and *"ahh"ed* over cherry blossom trees, which, when she takes them home, don't blossom, and don't produce cherries. Marvellous flowering bushes that *WOW* her with their full bloom, which, in her delicate hands, wilt and die. My mum, so kind and gentle, who lovingly and successfully managed to raise two human beings, somehow kills every plant she touches. But there is always an exception to the rule. In her case, it was a stunning rhododendron bush that has been growing and flowering so proudly in the corner of our front garden for as long as I could remember. My mother loved that plant, probably as much as she loved her own children. But one day, I came home from school to a very upset, almost frantic mother, all because of that rhododendron bush.

"Come on then, where is it?" she demanded, the second I walked through the door. Usually, I at least get to take my coat off before getting accused of things!

"Where's what?" I answered, a bit taken aback by her uncharacteristic outburst. Even when I had genuinely done something wrong, she hardly ever shouted or got too mad.

"You know exactly what I'm talking about!"

She stormed past me, out the front door like a teenager throwing a tantrum and I had to stop myself from laughing. By now my brother had heard the commotion and came to join us, but when I looked to him for an explanation, he shrugged, just as dumbfounded as I was. We followed her out the front door and found her standing in the front garden, staring down at a huge dugout hole in the soil.

"Well?" She demanded again, her eyes were fierce with anger and frustration.

I looked at the empty patch of soil and it took me a minute to realise the rhododendron that my mum was so proud of, was gone.

"What happened to that pink thing in the corner you love so much?" I asked, just as shocked as she was, but still no less willing to admit that I knew that it was called a rhododendron.

"You tell me? You've obviously hidden it somewhere!"

"You think I took it!? What?! That doesn't even make sense!"

My eyes shot to Dylan, did he put this in her head? Maybe he hid it to blame on me? In typical little brother fashion, he loved to get me into trouble, and this was a perfect example of the kind of stunts he would pull to do just that. But when I looked at him, he shot my bewildered look straight back at me, throwing his hands up in the air in defence. If he had done this, he wouldn't have bothered to lie about it. Rather he would be sniggering to himself behind her back. But this time, he appeared to be innocent. My mum stood, arms crossed, steam bellowing from her ears, waiting for my answer. I burst out laughing.

"Do you want to check my bag? My pockets, maybe? Come on! Where exactly do you think I've hidden it? Why on earth would I take it anyway?"

I could see my mum's brain ticking away, thinking that actually yeah, that was ridiculous. But still, she carried on.

"You *must* have taken it! Rhododendron bushes don't just vanish! You must've taken it as a joke. Well, fine, ha-ha very funny! Now, tell me where it is!"

Dylan and I looked at each other, wide eyed and shocked before we creased with laughter.

"Mum," I started in my most calming voice, once I stopped laughing. "I honestly don't know anything about this!"

She stared at me for the longest time, trying to pry out my lies. When I didn't budge, she let go of her gaze and sighed loudly. She began slowly circling the inner grass of the garden, studying the borders that were lined with other unimpressive plants trying their hardest to flower. She studied every inch, peering behind the other larger plants, making sure the rhododendron wasn't hidden behind one of them. After her second walk-round, she stopped in front of us again and let out another long sigh, the mark of defeat.

"Well then, I don't know!"

She threw her arms out and spun around, looking again for an answer.

"Did someone steal it?"

She looked back and forth between Dylan and I a few times before we realised it was not a rhetorical question.

"Oh no, I'm sure no one stole it!", "Oh no that's awful!", we quickly offered her.

She looked like a deer caught in headlights, so hurt at the thought that someone would steal her beloved rhododendron bush. We didn't know what else she wanted us to say. She just continued to spin around on the spot, frantically scanning the garden; I'm not sure for what, checking she hadn't missed the 3 feet wide plant hiding somewhere? Clues, maybe? Dylan and I looked at each other, shocked, partly that such an event could create such sudden turmoil and partly that someone would actually steal a bush from our garden!

"Well," Dylan finally stated, rather matter-of-factly for his age, "at least we'll get another trip to Dobbie's," he ended in sarcasm. He shrugged and retreated inside the house, no big deal.

Rather than continue to bellow in laughter at my poor, disgruntled mother, I had nothing left to do but follow my brother into the house and leave her to her spinning.

My brother and I have a pretty standard sibling relationship, which grew slightly more tolerable as we both grew older. For most of our childhood, my brother was my sworn archenemy. Growing up, I was pretty sure that his main purpose in life was to drive me crazy, something he did rather well. When we were kids, he would follow me around the house, chanting or singing at the top of his voice. He was relentless, unforgiving, and the most annoying little brat on the planet. He and his friends would break my stuff, scribble all over my sketchbooks. But the worst of all, if I so much as raised my voice to him, he would turn on the waterworks like a burst pipe, running to our dear mother that I had hit him. She fell for it every time.

It didn't take Dylan long to realise that he could use this at his advantage. It took all the willpower in the world to stop myself from smacking him across the head or kicking him in the shins every time I heard those evil words leave his smug little face, *"You can't touch me, you can't touch me. I'll tell Mum, I'll tell Mum"*.

He would sing at me with a twisted satisfaction as he watched me crumple with fury. A scene that usually ended with me screaming in frustration as I stormed away, leaving him to his pathetic little victory dance. A two-pronged celebration of both my defeat, and his safety. Sometimes, I just couldn't stop myself. The minute Dylan saw I was at boiling point; he would start screaming and crying as if I was torturing him. But I quickly discovered that raising my hand to Dylan resulted in the same punishment, whether that hand struck or not. I usually figured, if I'm going to get grounded either way, I might as well make it count.

Eventually, Dylan did learn that he would get his ass kicked either way, and eventually stopped crying wolf, making our brother-sister relationship a lot more tolerable – most days, at least.

*

Spending days at the local garden centre with my family was always a nice break from my own life for a few hours, but nothing could change the world I was living in the rest of the time. There were still thick, black clouds that seem to follow me wherever I go; there was still no colour. Even in those magnificent flowers I once admired, the ones that bloomed in bright pinks and incredible purples, this time around, I saw them differently. They were no longer magnificent; they were faded and pale. They were no longer incredible; they were washed out, like a painting that had been left out in the rain. The colours were draining away, and although I could still remember that the painting was once a beautiful masterpiece, it was now nothing more than a pool of muddied paint on the ground. I used to love flowers. There is something so pure, so honest about them. They are what they are, and they can't change that, or hide it, so instead, they flaunt it. Through all the clouds and the darkness and the pain, through all the things that I knew were missing from my life, colour was the thing that I missed the most. Something that my life no longer had any of. That summer, I grew to appreciate our trips to the garden centres. Something that Dylan and I had complained about throughout most of our childhood was now something that I looked forward to. I saw things differently now, but I still remembered how they used to look. And flowers will always smell like flowers, even when all the lights are off. When you lose one of your senses, you must learn to rely on the others.

Seeing the things I used to love so much, made me think of all things I would miss if I wasn't here. I thought about that sometimes. What it would be like just to give up. Lie down and go to sleep and just never wake up again. I thought that if my only other option is to continue living here in this darkness, then perhaps giving up would be the better option. But I knew that it wasn't an option. As much as I believed most days that nobody would really notice if I was gone, I knew in my heart that at the very least, my family would. Ending everything would be the easy way for me, but for them, it would destroy them and I just couldn't do it to them.

Knowing that there was no way out, made it all the harder to keep moving forward, from one dark day to the next.

Some days the thought of making it through the day to the next, seemed impossible. Some days, I wished I could kill myself. I wondered what would happen after, what would be waiting on the other side. I didn't believe in heaven or pearly gates, but there had to be something? There couldn't just be nothing. I imagined a world full of colours. I envisioned my soul leaving my body and looking down on a pale, grey, sickened figure of a body that is malnourished of anything good and positive. I saw my soul looking back through the darkness at my body and smiling in contentment as it floated through the dark to the other side. It was saying to me that it's ok, that it's better there. It is what my soul would want; to be set free, to move on to a better world.

When I imagine it, I find myself in a garden, surrounded by greens and pinks and blues and yellows. The yellows are so bright, I just want to taste them. I float over to the yellow petals, hanging graciously in front of me, and pull the flower softly from the branch and reach it to my lips. It smells so sweet, like sugar and honey and chocolate all in one. Now I am passed over to a new world, I can spend my time walking through this beautiful garden where I can taste the sweetness in the flowers, I can let the birdsong lift me up as I float through my garden without a care in the world. There are streams of clear, blue water and trickling waterfalls that cascades down the rock faces, making them glitter in the sun. And the sun, how I have missed the sun. Here, it shines so bright, yet it never burns. It touches everything with its light, and everything is perfect. This is the world that I long for, a world that is so out of reach. Until then, I must find some solace in the world I have now. But it is difficult, when everything is tainted.

I used to think about the things I would miss, if one day, I ran out of strength. It's the simple things I think, the things that can't be replaced. Things that no one else would understand. I would miss Sunday afternoons when my Granda would visit and would take sole ownership over the remote control, a grievance that Dylan and I were not allowed to argue about! We would sit like zombies, bored at the terrible TV shows we would be made to watch – *Countryfile, Songs of Praise*, black and white movies that we were too young to understand or appreciate. We would snigger together at my Granda's complete inability to hold a conversation. When we asked him a question or anything that required a response, for example, *"nice day today, isn't it Granda?"* we were highly unlikely to get a response. However, ask a second question, *"Would you like a cup of tea, Granda?"*, and he would happily answer the first, *"Oh yes, it's a lovely day!"*. We could never decide if it was because his trail of thought was so slow or if he just couldn't be bothered answering our questions.

I would miss Monday nights, family night. My dad's only night off and the only time of the week he verged on tolerable. We would be forced to spend the evening bonding as a family, playing Monopoly that someone always cheated at, or watching a movie that never managed to please everyone.

I would miss my mum yelling that tea's ready, I will miss the arguments in the morning about getting ready for school. All the things we take for granted in life, the things we don't notice until they're gone. I knew that when I was gone, they would be the things I would miss the most.

I remember the first time I ever thought about my death. I was about ten years old. My friend Elaine and I were on a romantic double date with our boyfriends, Harry and Simon; or as romantic as it can be at ten years old. After spending the evening loitering in some of our usual spots throughout the village, we decided to end our date with some romantic star gazing in the park. The four of us lay on our backs on top of the climbing frame in the middle of the park. I remember thinking how dark it was, being so far away from all the streetlights. The sky was lit with a million stars, twinkling gracefully above us. It was the first time I had ever noticed how beautiful the night sky could be, and I guess also, how beautiful the world could be. For a while we lay there quiet, silently breathing in the beautiful moment around us. We imagined our own constellations from the shapes the stars made and told stories of how they became frozen forever in that position. I guess none of us knew any actual constellations. We lay there, side by side, hands clasped, connecting us in our own private moment. At 10 years old, private time with the boy you like was few and far between. I remember feeling so close to Harry as I watched the warm puff of our breaths mingle in the cold air around us. It was the first time I had ever felt close to a boy. I remember thinking how beautiful the moment was and I wished I could stay in it forever. We were all so quiet that night, each one of us peacefully watching the stars above us play out their stories as they watched down over us. I remember it made me feel protected, like something, or someone was watching over me.

Suddenly, Elaine shouted, "Oh my God, look! There's a shooting star!"

We all sat up eagerly in unison, excited to see our first shooting star.

"There's another!" shrieked Elaine, pointing into the sky in another direction.

"And another!"

"And another!"

For a few moments, we all sat in wonderment, amazed at our luck to see not only one shooting star, but a whole sky full of them.

"This is crazy. Are there usually so many shooting stars all at once? Is this, like, normal?"

"Err…I kind of thought you only usually see one at a time."

"So, what the fuck is going on?"

"I have no idea."

We sat for a while, considering our new revelation, trying to decide whether to still consider ourselves lucky to have witnessed some freak act of nature, or to accept the possibility of our imminent death. I could tell from the increasingly worried faces around me, that our beautiful moment was over. Seeing fear consume the features of my friends set panic into my own chest. Suddenly, I couldn't breathe. I didn't get long to worry about it before Simon jumped down from the climbing frame.

"This is fucked up. Let's get the fuck outta here!"

"I'll walk you home. Don't worry, I'll keep you safe," Harry beamed at me, reaching again for my hand so we could jump down together. My breath returned.

We followed Simon without hesitation. We walked at a quick pace, fairly calm at first.

"It's probably just a whole bunch of shooting stars. Or maybe one star that burst into lots of little bits in space and now we're seeing the bits!"

But the more we walked, and the more stars we saw continuing to fall, the more frantic we became.

"So, where do falling stars go? Do they fall to Earth? Will all those stars fall to Earth? Won't they like, crush whatever they land on?"

"What if it's alien spaceships?"

"They're heading straight for us!"

At that, panic sunk its teeth into all of us and the four of us bolted in opposite directions to get home as fast as humanly possible before the aliens attacked/half of space fell on Earth, crushing everything in its wake! So much for Harry and I's romantic walk home to make sure I was safe.

Needless to say, we all made it home safe. Exploding stars did *not* crush everything around us and aliens did *not* invade. But in our defence, *Independence Day* had not long been released, and we were only ten. Make believe or not, that night will always go down as one of the most terrifying moments of my life. The four of us never talked about it again and I certainly never told anyone else about it.

Thinking that night that I was going to die, I was terrified. But now, I feel nothing.

Chapter 6 - A Whole New World

When I returned to school after summer, everything felt different. Most of the Shop-mob were gone and there was a sense of peace that seemed to flow throughout the whole school. It was as if the whole student body had let out a collective sigh of relief and now the whole building could breathe easy. I suddenly felt so much more connected to the rest of the world. Like their presence was keeping everybody apart, keeping everyone isolated and alone. But now that they were gone, everyone else had come together, uniting at the freedom this year would surely hold for us all. This year really was going to be different, hopefully I could be too.

But returning to school also brought with it an overwhelming anxiety about seeing Jamie again. It had been almost six weeks since he serenaded me on my doorstep, five and a half weeks since I may or may not have emailed him with my number, which he never called. I had spent the last six weeks sick to my stomach at the thought of seeing him again. Did he get my email and decide not to bother calling? Had he gone down south and met someone prettier, cooler than me and forgotten all about me? Did he regret turning up at my door altogether, embarrassed by his drunken misjudgement? Either way, it had taken me several weeks of outfit planning and preening to look perfect for our reunion on the first day back. This year, I had opted for an ankle length black skirt with a sexy but uniform appropriate slit up one side, paired with a low-cut black lace top that showed off my cleavage – a massive improvement since last time we saw each other. Imagine my disappointment to find out that he was still on holiday and wouldn't be back at school until the following week. It was going to be a long week.

Other than my utter disappointment and equal measure of relief at Jamie's no-show, the rest of the day was rather uneventful and not unlike any other day. I got up, grudgingly. I walked to school, nervously. I went to classes, uninterestingly. The most exciting part of the day came after lunch, with the first chemistry class of the year, when I met a boy called Tom.

One thing that I had actually been looking forward to this school year was chemistry. One of the few classes that I didn't completely hate and which I wasn't completely terrible at. Our teacher this year would be Mr Simpson. A popular teacher whose eyes sat in narrow slits behind inch-thick glasses, making them appear even more slit-like, awarding him the nickname *Mr Sleeps-a-lot*. Mr Simpson had a dark, completely unfunny sense of humour, which of course made him utterly hilarious. His style of humour was to be mean to people. He would ridicule people for wearing the wrong outfit and laugh along with the rest of the class if anyone made a fool of themselves. It sounds mean, but he knew how to pick his victims. He didn't pick on the geeky, insecure kids. He picked on the 'cool' kids, the ones that think they're untouchable. But when you're the teacher, you can pick on whoever you like; no one is untouchable. By picking his victims so wisely, he wasn't labelled a bully, he was crowned a hero.

I was last to get to class, just as I was with every other class. But since this was the first class of the term, being last to class also meant getting the last pick of seats available; often resulting in being forced to sit next to the smelliest boy in class or the most annoying girl, who will grass on your every wrong move. The worst part was, the seat you choose on the first day of class was yours for the rest of the term, and ultimately determined whether or not the class would suck.

The chemistry lab was arranged into small rectangular islands that fit four students to a bench. By the time I got to class, my friends were all secured into their places around two of the benches. In a class of only eight people, four of us were close, and anxious to sit together for the year. But when I arrived, someone else was already sitting in the fourth seat, *my* seat. And now, there was only one seat left, the seat next to him. To begin with, I thought he must be new, I'd never noticed him before. But he was not new; he had been there the whole time. But in the four years we had gone to the same school, in the same year, even in some of the same classes, I had never once noticed him. But that day, I felt a connection with that boy. A connection that I couldn't describe, with a boy that I'd never even met before.

I didn't think much of it at first. I was too busy sulking, pissed off that for the rest of year, all my friends would sit together, laughing at inside jokes that I wouldn't be part of, because I'm sitting at the back of the class on my own. At first, I hadn't even realised that he was sitting there when I plonked my bag down onto the bench in front of him and threw myself angrily into the stool directly across from him. I spent the next ten minutes wallowing in my own self-pity and hadn't so much as taken out my notebook. After a short reminder from Mr Sleeps-a-lot that this was actually a classroom and not a 'social gathering that I hadn't been invited to', I started to fumble through my seemingly bottomless bag in search of my chemistry book, which I quickly realised I didn't have with me. As I sat back, frustrated at myself and my lack of organisational skills, the boy sitting across from me, (who so far, I have failed to even acknowledge), without looking up, silently slid his book towards me. He surprised me, mainly because until now I had forgotten he was there. I thanked him. He nervously raised his head and his gaze fluttered quickly to mine, and then just as quickly, fluttered away again. That was it. That was all it was. We didn't so much as exchange words, but I felt something there, something in the air that I couldn't explain. I spent the rest of the day thinking about him, lost in thoughts of a boy that I hadn't spoken a single word to. But in those few seconds that my eye caught his, I saw a sadness that I recognised all too well; like I was looking in a mirror. There was a sadness in his eyes that cried out, pleading to be saved. In that one silent moment, I wanted to save him, this boy that I didn't know. And if I could save him, maybe he could save me too.

The next day, the hours dragged as I waited anxiously for chemistry class in the afternoon so that I could sit with Tom again. I managed a small 'hi' when I first sat down next to him. And I strained to hear the minuscule 'hi' that I got back in response. For the entire hour, I searched so hard for the words to say to him, but nothing came. I was so nervous around him, but I couldn't understand why. I was so fascinated by him, but I had no idea why. I studied his face while we sat in silence and I found myself wanting to memorise his every feature. There was something about him. Like there was an air around him, like an aura, that makes me need to know him. He didn't speak, he didn't even interact, not just with me, but with anyone, but it made him all the more intriguing. It made me want to know what he was thinking, what he was feeling. But the air around him was full of heartache and tragedy, like the whole world had fallen from beneath his feet. I knew the feeling, because I felt like that too some days, most days, like there was nothing around me but cold, empty air. But he didn't feel cold. He felt true, and loving, and loyal. But his eyes were empty, like there was nothing left. There was no strength left. I could sense it in him, because I recognised the feeling so well from within myself. I wondered if he could sense anything about me. Was he also thinking that he needed to know me, the way I needed to know him?

The next day, I was determined to try once again to find some common ground with Tom. I could sense that we could be something special to one another, but first, I had to find a way to talk to him. But Tom never turned up to class that day, or the next. I would have to be patient and wait to talk to him, something I was not very good at.

The following week, I finally got to see Jamie again. I never heard back from him after my (possibly) failed attempt at emailing him my number. I was still plagued with doubt that he even remembered my name and having to wait another week, didn't help any! I figured he'd probably met somebody else by now, someone much more tech-savvy than me, who knows how to send emails, no doubt. Or maybe he just wasn't really that interested in the first place. I couldn't blame him. *I* didn't even like being around me, so why should he? But as it turned out, he hadn't met anyone else, and he hadn't forgotten about me.

It was the end of lunch before I saw him. Our eyes met across the crowd and he flashed a smile at me that lit up the whole room. His eyes were so genuine, so kind. My heart raced as I saw him excuse himself from his friends and make his way through the crowd towards me. I felt panic stick in my throat, and I choked on the words I hadn't formed yet.

"Hey, you, remember me?" he beamed at me.

"Yeah, of course! How was your summer?"

I was so nervous. Lately, I had spent so much time concentrating on how terrible the world was and all the people in it, that I had almost forgotten what it felt like to actually *want* to talk to someone.

"Good." His eyes fell to the floor self-consciously.

"Didn't you get my email?" I rushed, there was no way I was going to tell him about my awful encounter with the internet, but I still needed him to know I was interested.

"No," he said hopefully.

"Oh, well I did send you one. I figured when you didn't reply that you were just busy or something. It's fine though." Now was my turn to look self-conscious.

"Oh no, I didn't get anything. I really did want to hear from you though," he rushed back at me, embarrassed that he seemed disinterested.

"Well, I'm here now, so if you still want to, you know, hang out or something, you know."

His words stumbled awkwardly, and I imagined them sticking in his throat the same way mine did. He blushed slightly and it seemed that maybe he wasn't all that familiar with these sorts of social interactions either. It made me feel better to think that he was as nervous and vulnerable as I was.

"Yeah, that would be nice," I replied.

I could feel heat stinging my cheeks and I knew I was blushing much more than he was. I looked away embarrassed and laughed nervously.

"OK, it's a date."

His eyes sparkled with excitement. He had such beautiful eyes. They were so brown that they were almost black, and I could clearly see my own reflection in them. Just at that, the bell rang, signalling the perfect end to a perfect beginning.

"Well, I guess I'll see you tomorrow, maybe?"

"I'll be here," and he flashed another amazing smile at me before turning and losing himself into the sea of people.

I stood there, dazed, enjoying the feeling of the butterflies swirling through my body in delight, rather than their usual state of panic. I couldn't remember the last time I actually looked forward to tomorrow. One conversation, one tiny moment in time and already I knew, this was going to be the start of something wonderful.

Despite the initial awkwardness, Jamie was surprisingly easy to talk to, and it wasn't long before we were spending every break time together. I was getting to know more and more about him every day and it struck me that I didn't know this much about any of my other friends. His biggest passion was classic cars and at the weekends he worked at a local car garage that specialised in the classics. Compared to most people in our village who had lived there their entire lives, Jamie had led a far more interesting life. He had lived here when he was young, but when his parents divorced when he was only five years old, he and his mum had moved to England to live with his gran. Jamie's mum eventually remarried, and they moved back to Scotland to 'start over', where he now lives in the neighbouring village a few miles away. Jamie's mum and stepdad started a new family and also have twin boys – Jamie's half-brothers. Although Jamie talked more openly than anyone I had ever met before, when it came to his family, he shut down. I wondered if he still felt part of the immediate family, or if he felt like a spare part, a left over from his mum's previous life that she couldn't throw away. I knew how hard it was to feel left out of my own life, but I couldn't imagine how it would feel to be left out of your own family. I didn't push him to talk; if nothing else, I knew how important it was to hide the parts of yourself that you didn't want anybody to see.

After about two weeks of becoming inseparable during school hours, it was finally time for Jamie and I to have our first date. I was so nervous. We talked constantly at school, but I was always waiting for the words to run out. One day, we would just have nothing left to say to one another. But so far, that day had never come.

Saturday night, we had planned to 'hang out, or whatever' at mine. Jamie's mum dropped him off at my house and as soon as I opened the door, I could see the sweat on his brow. I was relieved to see that he was just as nervous as I was. I have had boyfriends before, but this seemed different. This seemed like so much more than it ever had done before. Like this was the only one that counted. So, it had to be right.

As with any first date, the night got off to an awkward start and I started to worry that I had been right about the words running out. Thankfully, Jamie had come armed with a bottle of *Lambrini,* and it wasn't long before our Dutch courage took hold, and we were talking and laughing non-stop as if we'd known each other our entire lives. He made me feel as if I could finally breathe again. For so long, I had felt like I'd been locked in a dark room, with no light and no air. And now Jamie had turned up and unlocked me. Like he had drawn back the curtains and let the room flood with dusty sunlight. He opened all the windows and now the air that circled the room was crisp and clear and smells of summer. A summer that I thought was gone forever.

When he finally got up the courage to kiss me, I felt like summer would never end. His lips were so soft and so gentle against mine. I felt his touch radiate throughout my body, from my hungry lips, to the tips of my fingers, right down to my toes. As we kissed, he ran his hand up through my hair and down across my shoulders, resting his hand on the small of my back. I knew he wanted to move further, and I wanted him to. But for tonight, for now, it was perfect. Even hours after he had left, I was still tingling from the memory of the touch of his hand moving slowly down my back, of his lips so gently caressing mine. I never wanted it to stop. I had never felt this way before. For the first time in my life, I was in love.

After that night, Jamie and I truly became inseparable – day and night. It felt like we'd been together forever; like before him, there was nothing. But now there was something, everything, and after just a few weeks of knowing him, I couldn't imagine my life without him. We needed each other. He was my rock, and I was his. I'd had boyfriends before, and at the time, I always thought I loved them, but it was only now that I realised that I had never been in love before. This time was different; this was so much more than I could ever have imagined. Every inch of me was consumed, overwhelmed by my need for him. And everything else was gone. All the clouds dissipated; all the darkness had been entirely replaced by love. Being apart from him was painful. We spent every moment we could together, and it still wasn't enough. I hated it when he went home at the end of the night. I wished he didn't have to, I wished he could stay with me always. I wanted to know everything about him and him me. But as much as I wanted to let him in completely, to know everything about me, I couldn't. I wanted him to know everything. To the know the darkness that surrounded me, to hear the demons that whispered in my ear that the world was against me. *What if he thinks I'm crazy? What if he's right?*

For the meantime, the demons seemed to be at bay. Being with Jamie brought me a new light; a reason to get up in the morning, a reason to keep breathing. My whole life was different and now I had no reason to be unhappy. I was one half of 'Gill and Jamie', and having another half to complete me, I couldn't imagine that I would ever be lonely again, I was complete. When I started going out with Jamie, I was also accepted into a whole new social circle and suddenly found myself with more people around me than I had ever had in my life. *This is probably what it's meant to be like,* I thought. People say that your teenage years are the best years of your life, but so far, I hadn't been able to understand that. Years of darkness, desperation, isolation and self-mutilation, how could these be the best? But this must be it. This is what people mean when they say, 'Enjoy it. These are the best years of your life'.

As Jamie and I grew closer, he confided in me more and more. I felt so honoured that he trusted me enough to open his heart to me the way he did. It was as if he had been carrying these feelings for so long, never able to find anyone to help him carry them. On the outside, he seems so normal. He was the definition of 'happy-go-lucky'; he was fun, and easy and he seems genuinely happy to be alive. But the closer that I got to Jamie, the more I could see that there was so much more to him. I knew that behind all the laughter and jokes, there was sadness, just like there was in me. He reminded me of a rainy day. The days where it rains and rains, like it will never stop. And just when you think that it really will never stop, that you've lost all hope that you will ever make it outside again, suddenly, it stops. The sun breaks through the clouds, the beams bouncing off the wet ground and illuminating everything it touches. That's what Jamie was to me. He was the sun on a rainy day.

And when one night, he spilled out his story to me, like lava burning his lips, I felt proud. So proud that he was able to do something, which I knew only too well how hard it was, to trust someone with your heart.

When Jamie was five years old, he and his mum left his dad. His dad was violent. He said he didn't remember it much, just bits and pieces. He remembered hiding in his closet in his room upstairs, while downstairs his father screamed bloody murder at his mother. He listened to the sound of chairs being tossed in rage, glasses smashing. He didn't remember ever seeing the violence that his mother endured, but he heard it and he saw the bruises appear on his mother's face, on her arms and her stomach. He didn't understand it then, but as he got older, the reality of their situation became clearer to him and the jumbled memories started to piece themselves together. A few years after they left, he confronted his mother and she filled in the blanks that she'd spent so many years hiding from him. Jamie never saw any violence because his mum knew how to hide it. She sheltered him from his father's abuse. She sent him to his room the minute his father came through the door drunk, anticipating what would come next. She took beating after beating, so that Jamie didn't. Jamie's father never touched him, because his mother always stood in his way.

Eventually Jamie's mum remarried and started a new family, and they ended up back in Scotland, in a new house, not far from the house that he and his mother had left all those years before.

Jamie spoke for a while about his family, and I listened. He told me stories about his twin brothers and how they have a 'twin-thing' where they can communicate to each other without talking. He talked about how happy his mum is now with her new husband, who even though he had been Jamie's father figure since he was young, Jamie called him 'Harry', but never dad. He talked about how his mother doted over his younger brothers in a way that he never got to experience as a child. He talked about how happy his family were now, how he felt like they were given a second chance at happiness. Only, it didn't seem like Jamie ever got that second chance. Jamie's mum moved on and started again, only, she left her son behind, tagging along at the back, forgotten. Was she so wrapped up in her new family that she never noticed her first son being left behind? Did she blame Jamie in some way for what happened with his father? Did she wish that she had left him too?

He didn't admit to feeling left behind. But I could see it in his eyes that telling happy stories about his family somehow hurt him. None of those stories included Jamie. I thought maybe he was ashamed. I think in his situation, I would have been too. I would feel like I wasn't good enough. Like I wasn't loved or wanted.

Jamie started to hint that he had been having some issues at home with his stepdad, who according to Jamie, had a very low tolerance towards him in general. But when I asked Jamie if he ever got violent, Jamie quickly jumped to defence, swearing that Harry would never hurt his mum or the twins. So defensive of his happy family façade. I decided to drop the subject, thinking that Jamie had already opened up so much and probably wasn't ready for anything more. Then all of a sudden, he changed his mind.

'Just me. Just…a couple of times,' he blurted out so quickly, before he changed his mind about confessing.

He thought it was his own fault, that he deserved it. He thought he pushed Harry to the limit, and when he snapped and hit him, it was his own fault.

I didn't know how to deal with Jamie's situation. I didn't know what to say to him to make it any better. I couldn't give him the advice that he needed because I didn't have any. So, I did the only thing that I knew would help him. I let him talk until there was nothing left to say. Then I held him and told him that everything would be OK.

As much as I appreciated that Jamie had opened up to me, I just couldn't make myself do the same. I knew he was expecting me to – *I'll show you my scars, if you show me yours*. Only mine were literally scars.

Scars that once seeped blood across my forearm from the knife that I scored across it. My scars come from years of self-hatred for not being strong enough to shut out all the evil in the world and just carry on, like everyone else seemed to be able to do. He couldn't ever understand. It would be too much for him and I would lose him, the one thing keeping me from myself, I couldn't risk it. I wished so much that I could trust him the way I knew I should. But I couldn't talk to him. I didn't know how. I knew that he would look at me differently, just like everyone else did. I was sure that he already thought I was crazy. He had already seen the scars on my arms. I was usually so careful to hide that part of myself from everyone, but it's hard to hide something like that from someone so physically close to you. But I couldn't give him the explanation I knew he was waiting for. How could I explain it to him, when I couldn't explain it to myself?

I wanted to tell him everything. I wanted to be close to him, to let him be close to me. I didn't want us to have secrets, but I was so scared that mine were too complex for him to understand. It was best not to talk. It was best just to keep it all in where no one else can see. Jamie had his own problems to deal with, he didn't need to be burdened with mine as well. I loved Jamie with all my heart, but I'd given him everything I had to offer. And no matter how much I wished I could give him everything, I just couldn't. I was letting him down, just like I was letting myself down. I could feel my heart breaking more and more, every time I pulled away, not trusting. I knew he deserved more, more than I could ever give him.

Chapter 7 – A Boy Called Tom

A month into the new term and Tom finally reappeared in chemistry class, as if he had never been missing. Since I last saw him weeks before, I had continued to think about him; wondering where he was, and if I'd ever get to see him again. I was so unprepared for seeing him again that I hadn't given another thought to the words I wasn't able to find for him last time we sat together. Turned out, I didn't need to.

"I like your pictures," he said nervously, his eyes scanning the doodles and drawings sprawled all over my notebook.

"Thank you," I said back, shocked that after thinking about him silently for so long, he was finally speaking to me now.

When I looked over at Tom's notebook, I realised that the two could pass as a matching set. His book was even more covered than mine. Our drawing style was so similar, we even had some of the same images and band logos, only, his were better than mine, way better. I smiled back at him.

"I like yours too," I said.

"Thanks. I like to draw," he smiled at me, meeting my gaze. His blue eyes made my stomach flutter.

"Me too."

As Mr Sleeps-a-lot started the lesson and shushed the class into silence, I sat there numb, speechless, as if I had just met Johnny Depp. How can someone I don't even know make me feel like this? Especially when I was so in love with someone else.

I convinced myself that I was just excited to connect with someone new, that was all it was. I didn't make connections easily, and somehow, I had made a connection with Tom without needing to know anything about him. There was no reason why this should interfere with Jamie and I's relationship and no reason at all to avoid starting a platonic relationship with Tom. Because that's all it would ever be. He could still be someone special, just not in the same way that Jamie was.

The biggest of lies are those we tell ourselves.

*

Over the next few weeks, Tom and I's single-sentence conversations slowly blossomed into a real friendship. I waited anxiously each day for chemistry class so that we could chat and pass notes, and even draw pictures for each other. After discovering that we also shared an art class, I moved seats so that we could sit together there too. To begin with, people thought it was strange, that I moved away from my own friends to sit at another table, with a boy whose name they probably didn't even know. I was sure they were suspicious that I wanted to be closer to another boy when I was already with someone else. But I didn't care. In the hallways and between classes, I was spending all my time with Jamie. The classroom was the only place that Tom and I could spend time together. I felt so comfortable with him that I didn't care what anyone else thought, or even that there was anyone else in the room. I continued to tell myself that it was not the same as it was with Jamie. I loved Jamie and I loved being with him and I didn't want that to change. But when I was with Tom, I felt like nothing in the world could ever hurt me. And even if it did, Tom would be there to fix me.

Just as Jamie and I had been once, Tom and I had become inseparable. I still loved Jamie with all my heart, but now that the novelty of a new relationship had worn off, he seemed more interested in hanging out with his mates than me. I started to worry that we had already grown apart, that he was bored of me. But since I was spending most of my time now with Tom, I think it suited us both. Tom had fast become my best friend in the world. I knew I was right about him, right from the moment I first saw him, I knew. Jamie may have my heart, but Tom had my soul.

My favourite part of most days was art & design. Not only because it gave me time to spend with Tom, but also because it was the only subject I was even vaguely good at. For the 'design' part of the course, we had to choose a design concept, research it and produce a piece of artwork based on our own research of our chosen concepts. It was a rare opportunity where we were given permission to spend the entire class, out of class. How can one be expected to find a design concept that interests them if they do not go out and find one? So now the school atrium and grounds in general were littered with art students, with a genuine reason to be out of class, seemingly doing research. It drove the hall monitors mad. It was the first time Tom and I had ever spent any time alone. There was always someone else with us, which until now, had never even crossed my mind that we were missing out on something. But when we were alone, he was different, we were different. I felt like I was getting to see a Tom that nobody else knew but me. Like he was mine and I was his, and nobody else's. I spent all day waiting for our next art class together so that we could be alone together. I was plagued withguilt. It felt so wrong to want to be alone with another boy when I was so in love with another. But I wasn't in love with Tom, I just liked being with him. And when we were alone together, it was like there was nothing else in the world. Like everything else around us was just a distraction. But when we were alone, there were no distractions, there was nothing but us.

Tom had a deep sadness in him, possibly even deeper than mine. And like me, he had never confided in anyone about how he felt. I understood that completely. We never talked much about our own demons, but we didn't need to. Just for him to know that I had them, was more than I could say for anyone else in my life. Just to be around him, knowing that he understood me, what I was feeling, knowing that I didn't have to explain myself, was all I ever needed.

I wanted to feel that way with Jamie, but I just couldn't. I knew he would never understand. Tom understood without even having to use words. When I met Jamie, I thought the clouds had lifted. I thought it was over, and why wouldn't it be? The Shop-mob had moved on and my fear of leaving the house was easing every day that I didn't have to see their faces. I had a great group of friends and a gorgeous boyfriend who loved me. But was it all just an illusion? A distraction, luring me into a false sense of security, so that next time the storm came, it would hit twice as hard. I could feel it coming, just as strongly and silently as I could feel it easing. Shifting in both directions beneath my feet. It felt like the calm before the storm. But I always knew the storm would come, one day. And I knew that when it did, Jamie wouldn't be waiting on the other side. He would have blown away in the wind, just like everyone else. Just like everyone else always did. But Tom, I didn't need to know that he would be on the other side, because we were waiting silently together, waiting for the storm to come. He was already holding my hand, waiting to guide us through it, together.

One day, Tom and I decided to take our art research to a new level and managed to escape the school grounds. Tom told me what he was planning; he told me he wanted to take me someplace, someplace secret. I thought he was mad to even ask if we could leave school grounds, but somehow, Mr Lincoln said yes. We were gone before he could change his mind. Tom told Mr Lincoln that he was planning to study stone masonry and felt that a trip to the church graveyard to do some drawings of headstones and some grave rubbings would really help his project. I guess he told him that I wanted to do the same. In reality, neither of us had any idea what we would study. We had spent our art classes over the last few weeks doing nothing at all, just being together. We always made sure to throw together some quick five-minute sketch at the end of the period, as way of evidence that we had indeed been working for the last two hours. The last sketches we had each produced were almost identical and vaguely resembling a wooden bench, looking like it had been drawn by a five-year-old. Mr Lincoln was not impressed. But it had kept us amused for the rest of the day.

I didn't really understand why Tom would want us to spend the afternoon in a graveyard, so dark and full of death. When everyday life is already dark and full of death, why would he want to add to that? But when we got there, and we fell silent as we walked side by side between the tombstones, I understood. The graveyard was not full of horrors and death, it was full of people who are at peace. And what I didn't realise about peace, is that it's contagious. Tom led us over to a quiet spot towards the back of the graveyard, where we could sit on the grass with our backs against a low stone wall, taking in the sense of stillness around us. And for the first time in I don't know how long, I looked up to the blue skies above me and I felt the warmth of the sun spread across my face. I felt the grass beneath me. I smelt the wildflowers around us. I saw and felt, I remembered, just how beautiful the world could be, if you just let yourself see it. All my fears fell away from me, melted by the sun. The anger that had brewed so long inside me neutralised, overwhelmed by the feeling of calm in the air. I started to cry. I cried for the wonder of nature that I had missed so dearly. I cried in relief that that wonder still existed. I cried knowing that above all the dark clouds, the sun was still shining, even if you can't always see it. I cried because I missed the sun so much. I cried because although in that moment the sun did shine, I knew that soon it would vanish, and the world would once again be consumed in shadows.

I saw Tom shift instinctively to hug me. But before he reached me, he stopped, and pulled away. Instead, he moved to kneel in front of me so that we were face to face, just inches apart. He took both of my hands in his lap and gripped them tight in his. And without taking his eyes from me, he let me cry. He let me cry until I was finished. When I was done, he stood up, still holding my hands.

"Come with me. I want to show you something."

He pulled me to my feet with both hands and we stood for a second, hand in hand, facing each other. I felt so vulnerable, so naked with honesty. I had never cried like that in front of anyone before. But

I did, and afterwards, he was waiting to pull me back up from the ground. I had never seen Tom as strong before, but in that moment, all I could see was his strength – the strength he knew I needed from him.

Keeping hold of my hand, he guided me around the side of the church to a narrow passageway that ran along the back of the building. He told me that this was his favourite spot, that he came here when things got too much. It was a perfect viewpoint of the village. I could see the school and the thousands of houses surrounding it. I could see people in the streets like ants below us. I couldn't understand why he loved it so much.

"Look further," he said, sensing that I wasn't seeing what he could see. "Look past it all, right to the back of all those houses, what do you see?"

"Nothing. Just empty fields."

"Exactly. This place, where we are now, it doesn't go on forever. Beyond it, there is empty space. There is nothing."

He stared out longingly at the nothingness in the distance. "And from here, we are invisible. Like we're in a blind spot. I can see all of them in all their shitty houses, in their shitty lives. But they can't see us."

He turned back to face me. He picked up both of my hands in his again and squeezed them tightly. "So, when you need to, you can picture yourself here, invisible. You can picture us here, now, just like this, like there's nobody else."

His words echoed through my whole body and I felt the gap between us narrow. I could feel the warmth of his body so close to mine. My heart pounding to be so close to him. My body screamed for him to kiss me. And for a small moment, when our eyes met so purposefully, I saw that he felt it too. I saw a strength and determination in his eyes that I had never seen in him before. I felt it mirror in my own, like he was channelling straight to my heart. I felt him telling me something that he did not need his words for.

And then, just as quickly as it had happened, our moment was over. Reality grabbed hold and we fell back to earth.

"I guess we should go back."

"I guess so."

We walked back to school mostly in silence.

"It's like there's no one else." Tom's words played over and over in my mind all day. As he looked into my eyes as he said them, I melted, and I was his. Afterwards, I panicked. Tom was my best friend and that moment in the graveyard showed me just how much I needed him. But I wanted him to kiss me. I wanted him to kiss me and to never stop. But I loved Jamie, didn't I? How could I long so much for someone else, for my best friend to kiss me, to want me, when I was in love with someone else?

The next day, everything was different. Tom and I had always been able to somehow communicate without words, but there had never before been words that we weren't allowed to say. Now, the air between us was thick with all the things that we couldn't say. I was confused. I loved Jamie so much that it didn't make sense that I could have feelings for Tom. I did love Jamie. But Tom, he was everything. He was my heart and my soul, and I couldn't ever imagine being without him. Being with Tom made so much sense, yet it made no sense at all. I knew that he felt the same way I did. I didn't know what to do. All I knew was how beautiful his eyes were. When we first met, his eyes struck me with their sorrow, their pain. But now everything had changed. Now when I looked into his eyes, I felt them knock me to the ground. Crystal blue, flecked with deep green, like a clear Caribbean sea. And they were so deep, like a blue abyss that would suck you in and swallow you up if you looked too deeply. I could look into his eyes all day long.

The more I thought about him, about how much I longed for him to kiss me on that hilltop, the more I knew that it was right. Days later and I could still feel his fingers entwined in mine. I could feel fire rushing through my blood each time he touched me. I could feel the dense air between us swelling as we both willed it to dissipate and close the gap between us. I needed to be with Tom. I knew Jamie would be devastated. But I couldn't live another day without him.

*

Later that night, just as our household was getting ready to head to bed, Jamie showed up at my door. My mum, already in her pjs and dressing gown, answered the door to him. When she came through to my room and told me he was at the door, at first, I couldn't understand why she wasn't pissed off, him turning up unannounced late at night like this, normally, wouldn't have been acceptable. Instead, she looked worried. When I found Jamie on my doorstep, I could see why. He was standing in just a t-shirt, shaking. I wasn't sure whether he was shaking from the cold night or the raw emotion that seemed to be seeping from his pores. He looked as if the whole world had been pulled from beneath his feet. He didn't speak, he just looked up into my eyes, pleading, begging me to be there. So I was. I leaned out to him, took his hand and led him inside. As he came into the light, I noticed his lip was swollen and bloody. I didn't ask him what was wrong, I already knew. My mother was waiting with a blanket which I wrapped around him, hugging it close to him, trying to absorb some of the freezing air surrounding him. I assumed from the state of him that he walked the three miles from his house to mine, in only a T-shirt, in the middle of winter. He looked broken. My heart ached to see him so distraught. My mum re-entered the room, silently placing two cups of tea on the table in front of us. Mothers always know just what to do in these situations. As she left the room, he broke down. He crumbled into my arms and cried. All I could do was hold him up. Tears stung my eyes as his pain leached into me. I couldn't believe that anyone could do this to someone so harmless. With everything else that had been going on lately, I had almost forgotten how cruel the world was that we lived in. I had known of Jamie's family problems for a while, but I had never seen them up close. When his tears ran dry, I pulled his face to mine and ran my fingers around his chin, around the outline of his swollen pride.

"He did this?"

Jamie's eyes shot to the ground, trying to hide the shame in them.

"What about your mum? Couldn't she stop him?" I felt myself getting angry.

He shook his head, shocked. "She said it was my fault."

I felt myself double in pain as I absorbed his. She was his mother; her sole purpose in life should be to protect him. I pulled him to me tightly and cradled him, the way his mother should have done. The way I knew that my mother would if I needed her to.

Jamie's stepdad had turned out to be no different from his real dad. After years of enduring an abusive marriage, Jamie's mum had left his dad when the violence got too close to her son. Jamie grew up watching his mum beaten and abused, knowing that her abuse was the only thing preventing his. When she started to fear for Jamie's safety, she left. Now years later she is remarried and life, as it has a habit of doing, is repeating itself. Only this time, it is Jamie taking the abuse. I knew it had happened a few times before, but when Jamie talked about it before, he made out like it wasn't a big deal. I guess I didn't realise it was either. But seeing him that night, broken, crying in my lap like a little boy, I saw that the bravery he had always relied on had crumbled.

"I can't stay there anymore. I have to leave," he said suddenly, I could hear in his voice that his shock had been replaced with anger.

"Leave? Where to? Where will you go?" My anger was replaced with fear.

"Fuck knows. Anywhere. I'll get a flat in town. Get a job. I just, I just can't go back there!"

He gripped his head in his hands like he was trying to stop it from exploding. Waves of fear rushed through me at the thought of losing him, at the thought of him being alone. I saw Tom's face flash before me like a ghost. A betrayal. But before I had a chance to process the situation unravelling in front of me, he gripped my hands tightly in his and stared intensely into my eyes.

"Come with me."

"What?" I didn't know whether to laugh or cry.

"Come with me. Let's go, together. We'll get jobs, get a place together. Let's just get the fuck out of here!" His grip and his gaze softened, and I was reminded of the loving, caring Jamie that I fell so completely in love with not so long ago. "Think about it. It would be amazing. Just you and me. And nobody else."

Just as I was starting to melt into him, his last words stung me back to reality. Tom.

As I stared back into Jamie's eyes, I saw the boy I'd fallen so fast in love with was still there. Recently we had drifted apart. It's too easy to forget why you came together in the first place. He was still there, and he needed me. How could I ever think of leaving him when he needed me so much?

"OK," I told him.

My heart leaped at the thought of being with Jamie forever. He leapt over and hugged me, so excited at the thought of our new life together. But as he held me, as I faced away from him, a tear rolled down my cheek, laced with betrayal.

My mum let Jamie sleep on the couch. She said she would talk to my dad when he came home and sort it out. We didn't tell her that we already had a plan. That could wait until tomorrow. Maybe by then, we'd have come up with a new one.

Chapter 8 – Forever Bound

The next day, my parents called a family meeting and before long, Jamie's parents were in our living room, discussing with mine, how best to deal with the 'situation'. Despite my parent's best efforts, it didn't stay civilised for long. It was the first time I had met Jamie's mum and stepdad, and it was easy to see what Jamie was so desperate to get away from. Jamie's mum shouted and cried that he was destroying their family and that she just couldn't take anymore. She constantly contradicted herself. One minute he deserved the beating he took from his stepdad because he had brought it on himself, and the next, he had made it all up and her beloved husband had done nothing but treat him with love and patience. Jamie's own mother thought that the best thing for their family would be for him to leave home. Jamie's stepdad didn't say a word, silently relishing the drama that played out before him, as his wife took his side over her own son's. After seeing their reaction, or rather their lack of reaction to their son's grief, there was no doubt in my mind that Jamie was doing the right thing by leaving, and my own parents could see it too. And I knew I was doing the right thing by staying by his side. All his life Jamie has been abused, and now abandoned and I wouldn't be the next person in line to do that to him.

When we told our parents that our plan was to move into town and get a flat together, I expected my dad to be in agreement. I almost fell off my chair when my dad suggested that as a compromise, Jamie could move in with us. I was fairly certain that my dad didn't even want *me* here, never mind Jamie. As long as I could remember, my dad had never shown any sign that he cared about anyone other than himself. Yet somehow, he seemed to be trying his best to help Jamie out of his situation. My mum had very little to say on the matter, but I assumed that they had already discussed it at length – more likely, it was my mum's idea, in order to stop me from leaving home. Jamie's parents also had very little opinion on the wellbeing of their son, almost seeming relieved that he would now be someone else's problem.

So, we came to a compromise that Jamie would move in with us and would share a room with Dylan. We agreed to stay in school until the end of the year and in May, when the school year ended and we had done our final exams, we would both move out without any argument. A fair compromise, I thought. Both sets of parents continued to argue about money and logistics but by then, Jamie and I were so excited about the start of our new life living together, that a bomb could have gone off in the next room and I doubt we would have noticed. We would be together all the time, forever. It's all we ever wanted.

When my parents told Dylan what was happening, obviously worried at his reaction to having to share his room, they were relieved to see that he was just as excited as we were. Dylan and I had never gotten along and I'm sure he always wished he had a big brother rather than a sister, so really, he was getting his wish too. He was also excited at the idea that since the two boys would be sharing a room, they would need to move into the bigger bedroom – my bedroom. And I would be evicted, and moved into Dylan's boxroom – that part, I wasn't looking forward to. But if it meant that I could fall asleep knowing that Jamie was just on the other side of the wall, I would have happily slept in a cardboard box.

Once our parents had hashed out all the finer details, Jamie's mum and dad were more than happy to head along home without their son, leaving him in our care. Jamie and I spent the rest of the night just holding each other. This was the start of our new life together. We spoke about how amazing it would be, now that he wouldn't have to leave to catch the last bus home. He wouldn't have to wait to see me until after family dinner time. We could be together always, and we wouldn't even ever need to leave the house. We spoke about what would happen in May, how we would leave together and get our own place, make it into a home. We would decorate it however we wanted with scatter cushions and throw rugs and a funky retro clock for the kitchen. And one day, we would get married and have a family of our own and everything would be perfect. I could see it already. I went to bed that night with images of Jamie coming from work in his shirt and tie and his briefcase, after a long day at the office, working hard to provide for his family. He would come through the door just in time for dinner and I would pull out a steaming roast from the oven that filled the kitchen with scents of rosemary and love. I was dreaming of being a wife and I couldn't wait. I had no doubt in my mind that we would be blissfully happy together forever. And as for the moment I had with Tom, it would need to stay just that, a moment. Jamie and I would have a lifetime together. It was already planned.

Over the next few weeks, Jamie and I grew closer again and things began to go back to the way they were when we first fell in love. At home, we couldn't have been happier. Other than when we got sent to our separate rooms at 11 p.m. for bedtime, we were together all the time, all day, every day. We were so happy in our own little bubble that we hardly ever went out – which suited me fine. Things at school had improved so much since the Shop-mob left, but at night, it was a different story. You never could tell who might be lurking around the corner. And there were still certain areas of the village that I wouldn't go near. I never did tell Jamie how much I hated going out, but now that we both had another reason to stay in, I didn't need to. I didn't have to make excuses why I didn't want to walk past the shop after dark or why we should take the long way around so that we didn't have to walk down that long, dark lane that had no escape route, should anyone start walking towards us. Now we could just stay home and breathe easy.

But since we had stopped going out so much, we started to smoke a lot more weed. It was something that we often did at the weekend, everyone did. But recently, it had become a nightly habit. Every moment we got, we smoked. We were drowning in smoke, but at the time, I wouldn't have had it any other way. When you are in pain all day long, you need to find some pain relief. So far, getting high was the only thing that had ever worked. And it was just a little bit of weed, it wasn't doing any harm, was it?

Every day after school we would rush home and barricade ourselves in my room before setting up the bong. We would fill our lungs with the smoky analgesic, holding the smoke in as long as we could before dispelling the toxic smoke out the window, whilst holding onto the relief that flowed through every muscle in our tense bodies. We would lay on the bed, enjoying the waves washing over us, sending us both off into another world. A world without pain, without anger. A world where there was nothing but us. When I was in pain, my thoughts were fizzy. They were full of hatred. I spent my days forced to interact with a world that I didn't want to be part of, a world that wanted me there even less. Even those that called themselves my friends, I didn't trust them to be true to me, and my thoughts, my 'inner demon', only spurred me on. I could hear them whisper in my ear constantly.

They think you're an idiot. They think that you don't know. But you do know, don't you? You know how they conspire against you every time your back is turned. They are doing it right now. You hear their whispers when they think that you can't. You see their satisfied grins, but you know, they are smirking because they think they have fooled you. But they haven't fooled you. You know that you can't trust them. You can't trust any of them.

I couldn't even trust Tom anymore. After Jamie moved in, the space between us grew cold and wide. We still spend our time at school together, but I could feel the resentment hanging in the air all around us. *Everyone else can see it too. They have warped his mind against you. He is one of them now. You will only hurt him; you cannot be trusted. You do not deserve him. How do you think they would react if you died? Do you really think anyone would care? If you took that one last step off the edge and left them, just like you know they want you to, would they care? Would they even notice?*

During the daytime, my thoughts were like poison. But the night-time belonged to Jamie and I, and our cloud of serenity. I wish I could stay in this cloud forever.

*

For a while, things seemed to be improving and I was feeling much more at ease with myself. Now that we were getting high on a nightly basis, I only had to make it through the daytime. Each day, when school finished and I could hide away in my bedroom, I could be released into another world. A world of my own choosing and my own design. I only had to make it through the daytime.

During the day, I was still alone. I had Jamie of course, but I missed my best friend. Tom and I hadn't properly spoken since the day I cried in his arms at the graveyard. And when it was decided for us that Jamie and I would live together, sealing our fate to stay together, Tom and I never spoke of that moment again. As the weeks passed by, the space between us grew wider until I could no longer reach him at all. With everything that had happened with Jamie, I knew that I could never be with Tom. But I still wanted him to stay my best friend, I still needed him just as much as I always did. But I knew it was hard for Tom too. He grew cold and distant, until I barely recognised him. I hated him for leaving me, but I hated myself even more for missing him. I wanted more than anything for him to speak to me again. I didn't know how to speak to him anymore. I wanted to try, but my mind was so conflicted that I didn't know how to, not without complicating things even more. I wished that he would try, so that I wouldn't have to. Then one day, after months of silence, he did.

We were in chemistry class, where although we have moved apart emotionally, we still sat together. Now that our art field trips were over, chemistry was the only place we had left where we could be together without all the prying eyes of our friends and of Jamie, without people judging whether we were too close. But now, that closeness was painful. Now, when we talked to each other, the words were sharp.

"Hi," he said coyly as I sat down next to him, his eyes not leaving his page.

"Hi," I replied bitterly.

"I drew something for you."

He lifted his notebook and slid the piece of paper hidden beneath it towards me. I looked up at him so that he could see the distaste in my eyes. He was already looking at me, waiting to meet my gaze, but today his eyes were not hurtful, they were pleading. I felt my stomach turn and my whole body softened towards him. One kind look, that's all it took, and I was his all over again. I turned over the paper. It was a caricature of Freddy Krueger, both our favourite horror movie villain, holding out an oversized flower. In the days we were still close, Tom drew numerous Freddie's for me, some sketches in funny poses and some absolute works of arts. I treasured every one of them. I could feel my eyes sting with tears as the gesture shot me straight back to how we once were.

"I miss you," he choked.

I tried hard to hold my poise, I didn't want him to know how alone I'd been without him and how, now that he had come back to me, I felt like could deal with anything. I had missed him. But it wasn't until that moment that I realised quite how much. Over the last year, I had become especially good at lying to myself. So much so, that I didn't even know I was doing it. Tears rolled down my cheeks and I quickly swatted them away, embarrassed. I nodded softly to him.

"I miss you too."

All I wanted to do was hold him. I wanted to grab him close to me and never let go. Having Tom beside me made me stronger than any drug ever could. But before I could do anything, he slid another piece of paper towards me.

"I drew this one for you too."

Another Freddy.

"And this one. And this one. And this one."

Freddy drawings spilled out onto the table in front of me. I couldn't help but laugh, overwhelmed at such a simple, yet effective gesture, that no one else in the world would have understood but me. He had drawn me seven Freddys, evidence that I had been as present in his mind, as he had been in mine. He always was present in my mind. And as much as I tried to deny it, I had never stopped thinking about him. It was clear to me now, that I had never stopped loving him either.

Chapter 9 – The Darkness Returning

Tom and I were finally reunited, and our friendship continued as if it had never ended. We both had to accept that friendship was all we would ever have and the words that hung in the air once before, the words that we were not allowed to say out loud, still hung, clear as day. But after spending months apart, I think we both accepted that friendship, was better than having nothing at all. Jamie and I were now destined to be together forever, so any thought I had of being with Tom, I had to leave behind. And he had to do the same. It was hard, painful even to be around him and to be so forbidden to touch him the way that I so wanted to, it only made me want to touch him more. But having him as my friend, my best friend, was far better than not having him at all.

Jamie too was happy to welcome Tom back into the fold. He never did ask why Tom and I went from being so close to barely talking, but I always suspected that he knew, but just didn't want to know. More words, that hung in the air but were never said. But now that Tom and I were no longer spending time alone (in fact we were trying not to) and were no longer trying to spend to apart, we seemed to have become a threesome. Jamie accepting that Tom and I wanted to be closer than we were, and Tom and I accepting that we would only ever be friends. It was a little dysfunctional, but it seemed to work for everyone. In the few months Jamie and I had been living together, he had changed. He was not the boy I fell in love with. All he ever wanted to do was get high or drunk, and it didn't seem to matter to him whether I was there or not. So, it worked out fine for everyone. I got to spend more time with Tom, and Jamie and I never had to spend much time alone.

I worried about where our lives were heading. Our nightly routine of getting high was spreading, smothering most of our time together in a cloud of thick, relentless smoke. We very rarely went out at all, too comfortable shut inside our own worlds within the confines of my bedroom. We smoked every chance we got. Between classes, during our lunch hour, after school, before bed. I loved it, too much. The cloud we were living on was so soft and the thickness of the smoke acted as a barrier between me and the rest of the world, which is all I ever really wanted, to be as far apart from the rest of the world as I could. But when we weren't smoking, Jamie had become mean and aggressive, like he was angry at the fact that he had been forced to come back to earth for a while. He got so angry sometimes, that there were times I felt afraid of him, never knowing how he was going to react. Sometimes he would lose his temper for the smallest things. Like when he burnt his toast one morning and he stormed straight back into his room, where I found him punching his pillows so hard as if they had ruined his life. Or the time our dealer let us down and our weed supply ran dry for a day or two and when I went to hug him, to calm him down before he erupted, he pushed me so hard into a wall that my elbow pushed through the plasterboard and left a hole in the wall. He was always careful not to let anyone else see his aggression; that was just for me. But he was always sorry afterwards, and I always forgave him. He was only wrestling his own demons, the same as I was. Only he was doing it in a different way. Even still, I began to prefer it when there was someone else around, so that I wasn't alone with him. When it was just Jamie and I, I never knew which Jamie I was going to get.

After a few months of shutting ourselves away, refusing to leave the comfort of our own bedrooms, some of our friends eventually managed to convince us that we should start going out more. Nights were getting lighter and warmer and the excuse of avoiding the cold nights was running dry, now that spring was here. We had been spending so much time hanging out in my room that I was getting to a stage where I was scared to go out again. We hadn't purposely stayed in; it was just easier that way. When you're living in a cloud like the one we lived in, you want it to be warm, and have food. Outside didn't have those things. But I had never considered that the longer we put off going out, the harder it would be once we had to do it.

At first, I was terrified. As soon as we turned out of my street, I felt my chest seize tight, squeezing all the breath out of my body. My heart raced, quickly forcing blood to my frozen extremities. I was so ashamed of my irrational panic that I daren't tell anyone. I knew that it was irrational, but that didn't make it any less true. *They're going to get us, it's not safe out here! -Don't be so fucking ridiculous.* But eventually I realised that I had nothing to worry about. When we did go out, we went out in a group, if we did come across anything or anyone that actually warranted panic, we had each other. I would never have dreamt of going out alone. But I wasn't alone. I was with friends, and they would never let anything happen to me. Safety in numbers.

I was trying. I was pushing myself harder than I ever had before. Just trying to be normal. I knew in my rational mind that there was nothing to fear, that the idea of not going out just in case something *might* happen was completely ludicrous, I knew that. And I was trying so hard to defeat that thought. But it was all-consuming. I was exhausted, forcing myself not to be afraid all the time. Whenever I heard someone walking behind me, I would pray for my life. When I heard voices approaching, I would sink deeper into the shadows, hoping they would pass over me. I was exhausted, but I was doing it. And every time I did, it got a tiny bit easier.

Then one night when we were out, the world showed me that I was right to be afraid. I let my friends convince me that it was OK, that none of them would have let anything happen to us, but it did anyway. *I told you it wasn't safe! But you wouldn't listen!* I fell quickly down an agoraphobic spiral, straight back to where I started. There were people out there to hurt us. They're out there, searching for us, just so they can hurt us. I always knew it, but nobody would listen. But when the Shop-mob boys attacked Jamie, I knew I had been right all along. *It isn't safe.* Usually, my hypersensitivity can pick up another life form within about a 200-metre range, but I never even saw them coming. I let my guard down, I should have been protecting him. It was my fault. I should have fought harder to keep us inside, where I knew it was safe.

Jamie's attack hit me just as hard as my own did years ago. I tried to keep them away, but flashes of violence smothered my thoughts. I could feel every punch, every time, straight into my gut like a gunshot. Jamie seemed completely unaffected. He wasn't hurt, but then neither was I. Not physically, at least. Emotionally, it tore me to shreds. For me, it was the beginning of the end, an unravelling of hope for a world that I now knew was hopeless all along. Jamie was shaken at the time, but now he was just angry. He talked casually of plotting his revenge, as if someone had pulled a cruel prank. The boys spent the remainder of the night laughing and joking about ways in which they can get them back. It upset me even more that they could be so dismissive. Something terrible happened tonight, again. How could they be so casual about the fact the world is a cruel, evil, relentless place? How could they possibly be so happy to live in such a place? *Why can't anyone else see it?*

After Jamie's attack, we stopped going out again, and people stopped pressuring me to try. Fear had taken hold of me entirely and now it was the only emotion I had left, everything else was gone. I felt like there was poison seeping from my brain, into my blood stream. Before Jamie's attack, I was ashamed to admit that I didn't feel safe out there. But I should have been stronger, I should have fought harder. If I had, it would never have happened. Since that night, the boys who attacked Jamie started to make him their personal target. At school, he was suffering them every day; being pushed into lockers, tripped up in the hallways. It broke my heart to see him hurt. I hurt for him. I hurt for every person who had ever felt pain at the hands of another person. My thoughts were consumed with other people's pain, and I was in agony all the time. My insides screamed in pain.

But soon, the fear turned to anger. The anger that grew inside of me bulged at every seam. I could feel my blood, red hot, burning my veins as it drove adrenaline through my body. I had tried so hard all these years to survive this world. What if I no longer wanted to try? Not because I didn't want to live, but because I didn't want to live *here*. How could I want to live in a world so full of pain, so full of hatred? All these years I thought that *I* was the problem, that *I* wasn't strong enough to cope with what the world threw at me, that I was not brave enough to ride above it. But now I knew, it wasn't me that was the problem, it was the rest of the fucking world. *I can't fix this.*

Jamie didn't care. He laughed it off and dismissed it like it was nothing. He dismissed me, like my fears were nothing. He didn't understand. I always knew that he wouldn't. That when it came down to it, he didn't know me at all. For so long, I thought that things were getting better. But now, I could see that there would never be an end. My blood boiled in rage, my muscles were weak with fear, my heart is exhausted with despair at a problem that could never be fixed, a world that could never be saved.

Until now, I hadn't cut myself in so long, but now, it was the only thing that was keeping me alive. It's all I wanted to do all the time. When I wasn't cutting, I was waiting for the next time. Like a sweet addiction I couldn't live without. It's ironic, that causing myself pain, an act of violence against myself, was the only thing saving my life.

Every time I cut, I could feel the angst, the fear, and the hope seeping out of my skin, thick and dark like the blood that carried it. I wanted the hope to leave me. It was holding onto that hope that was hurting me the most. I, though, when it is gone, will be at peace, and I can leave here knowing that I have left nothing behind. No second guessing and no regrets.

That same week I went to see my GP. I knew something was wrong, I just didn't know what. I had read recently about brain tumours that can cause the chemicals in your brain to change, and it can make you think and do crazy things. *Maybe that's what's wrong with me, maybe I'm crazy? There aren't really people out to get me, are there?* I knew that I sounded crazy, but I couldn't control it. I felt like there was poison running through my mind, corrupting my thoughts, turning me against the rest of the world. It couldn't be true that the world was this cold. *It just can't be.* There had to be another reason. *At least if I have cancer, I will be dead soon. Then this will be over.*

I told my doctor that I wanted to have a head scan to check for a brain tumour. She told me I didn't have cancer and prescribed me antidepressants.

Why will nobody listen to me?!

*

As the school year dragged on, I was getting closer and closer to starting a new life. Part of me couldn't wait to get away. But the other part of me didn't want to leave. Jamie and I no longer seemed to be fighting for the same side and I didn't know if leaving together would make us stronger or break us apart completely. I wanted to believe that things would be different once we were gone. Maybe it was just what we needed, a fresh start together. Away from all the fear and all the anger. Somewhere we can just be ourselves, somewhere where we could feel safe again.

I wanted so badly to leave, to start a new life, but secretly, my heart was breaking. I knew that for Tom and I, it would be over, Tom and I both knew it. I felt nauseous at the thought of losing him, but I always knew eventually I would. My future was laid out before me, and there was nothing we could do about it. For months we had fought so hard to overcome our feelings for one another in order to hold onto our friendship, but what would happen when I am gone? When we won't see each other every day. When we have the option to take the easy way out and go our separate ways. I knew which option he would choose. I knew that when I left, I would be leaving him as well. All this time, I still held on to the small hope that one day the world would right itself, and we could be together. All he ever needed to do was say the word, and I would be his. But when school ends, and I start my life with Jamie, our time will have run out. We both knew that time was running out, but were both too afraid, both too sure of what we thought the future was *meant* to hold for each of us, unwilling to disrupt it. I could feel it in the air between us. I could hear it in-between all the words that neither of us could say and probably never would. In the weeks leading up to the end of term, I cherished every moment we shared together. He called every night at 11:10 p.m., knowing that by then, Jamie had retired to his own room. To begin with, being separated from Jamie at 11 p.m. was torture, and every night we fought for an extra half hour together. But by now, there were no arguments. Now, I spent the evening counting the minutes till the phone rang. By the time it did, I was already tucked up in bed, waiting to smother the ringing beneath my pillow so no one would hear it but me. I spent all day waiting for the only time I got to spend alone and uncensored with the boy I loved, but could never tell. The distance of the phone lines made us brave. We said things to each other that we would never dare say in person. Like talking in the dark, where no one can see your face. It was safe, the darkness concealing all the words that were spoken that shouldn't have been. Each night he sang me to sleep. His soft voice swaying me gently into a dream where I wasn't sure if it was real or if I had already drifted into a dream. It felt like a dream. A dream that I never want to wake up from. When I was listening silently to the notes of his voice caress me, the only way in which he was able, I never want to leave. I would have stayed there forever, just for the chance to listen to his voice love me each night.

A month before the end of our final school year, Jamie and I signed the lease to our new flat. Vowing, as promised, to move out of my family home as soon as we finished school. That same day, my dad also vowed to move out. It was quite a shock to say the least. I guess I also thought that people with separated parents would have witnessed their demise. There would be fighting and shouting and crying, and when they finally gave up and parted ways, there would be relief. But there was no fighting or shouting, I barely remember my parents ever even talking. I guess I always thought that if my parents were ever to split up, I would have at least been expecting it.

But there was no crying or shouting, just disbelief. I wasn't sad that my dad was leaving. I had no doubt that our family would be happier without him. There would be no sneaking about, no walking on eggshells, but then I wouldn't be there anyway. But as we sat as a family, to be told the news that we were now broken, I didn't see relief sprawled across my mum's face, I saw fear. I saw loneliness. In that moment, I've never loved or needed to be with her more. But instead, I will leave her too.

Chapter 10 – Let's Get This Party Started

Just a few days after finishing school forever, Jamie and I were excited to be starting our new life together and finally moving into our own place. For the first time ever, we could do whatever we wanted, whenever we wanted. We would leave behind all of the fear, all of the dangers lurking in the shadows, because in this new life, this new *adult* life, there was nothing to be afraid of and nothing that would ever hurt us again. And we would be together, falling in love all over again, while we started a new life *together*, a whole new fresh start.

My dad drove Jamie and I to our new home, not to make sure that we got there safely or to help us with our incredible amount of luggage, but to make sure we were really gone. At the time, I was so shocked at how our car journey went down, that for the first time in my life, I understood what people meant when they described themselves as speechless. My dad used the 45-minute drive as a soapbox, spouting out any hateful thought that came to his mind. I was so shocked, that I couldn't keep hold of his words, losing them to a fog of hurt in my mind. They swirled around us like shards of glass, cutting down any hopeful thought that we carried with us, tearing gashes like open wounds in the air around us. My dad spent the entire journey describing in grave detail, all the reasons why Jamie was responsible for the breakdown of his marriage. He relayed count after count, example after example of all the things we had done and said to weaken my parents' bond to breaking point, eventually causing it to snap. *"Jamie had no business encroaching on our happy family. Him being there had caused such a strain on our household that it caused me and your mum to fight constantly. The upheaval he caused wasn't fair on anyone including Dylan, who was forced to share a room with a stranger, causing him disruption in his life also. How selfish Jamie could be to have burdened our family with his own problems, when he is clearly not our responsibility. No wonder his own family didn't want him."*

It went on and on. Neither Jamie nor I muttered a single word in dispute. We both sat stunned, letting my dad's reign of fire burn through everything that had happened between us over the past year. At one-point, Jamie turned to me, his big brown eyes like a deer caught in the headlamps *"Do you feel this way too?"* he silently pleaded with me. But when he saw my expression mirrored his own, he no longer needed an answer. Then his expression changed. I saw the light go out in his eyes. He turned away, staring straight ahead into the distance, and he reached for my hand across the back seat. He held my hand as if he was holding on for his life; like he was falling inevitably to his death.

When it was over, we did not shout that he was wrong, that *he* was the problem. That every problem my family had ever had, was in fact because of *his* intolerance to human nature. Instead, we politely thanked him for the lift and let him drive away.

For all the problems that Jamie and I had between us, I could never fault the way that he integrated seamlessly into our lives and into our family. My brother saw him as the brother he never had. Dylan wasn't disrupted by Jamie's presence; he was elated by it. At times, when they were engrossed playing *Tony Hawk's* together, I actually found myself jealous; jealous that they were developing a bond closer than what Dylan and I had ever had. And I knew that my mum was always happy to have him around. My dad was hardly ever home. He worked long shifts that allowed him to spend as little time with his family as he possibly could, something that worked for all of us. I always got the impression that Dylan and I hadn't turned out to be exactly what he wanted us to be, and for that, he was resentful, and distant. He was hardly ever home, and it was only when he was, that there was any strain. When it was just Jamie, Dylan, Mum and I, things were great, like a family should be. We laughed more together than I think we ever had done. Jamie brought an ease to our house, a light. It was only when my dad came home that there was any tension. You could feel it in the air. We would hear the front door open and immediately, the air would tighten. It was like being in a room with a sleeping lion. It may look peaceful and harmless in its slumber, but at any moment, that lion could wake and tear everything in the room to shreds. Every step is a tiptoe. Every voice is a whisper. Fear of waking the sleeping lion creeps into everything you do. The obvious solution would have been to go out, to avoid home. But when you're just as terrified of the world outside as you are the world inside, where is there left to hide?

The first night at the flat together was wonderfully weird. My dad's revelations about Jamie of course put a dampener on things, but we were determined not to let it spoil our first night of freedom together. Once we turned the key to our new front door, and walked into our new home, and our new life, he was quickly forgotten about, for the meantime at least. On that first night, we weren't going to let anything, or anyone bring us down. We unloaded our bags and boxes into our new home and shut the door on the rest of the world for the night. Our first time properly alone together. We decided that this night would be ours and ours alone. We would celebrate with the masses tomorrow.

I was so excited for our first night together. I imagined the most romantic, magical night. Candlelight and rose petals and wine. This would be the first day of the rest of our lives together and just the chance we needed for us to remember why we fell so deeply in love in the first place. But in reality, it was…quiet. When we shut the rest of world out, all the sound went with it. We were suddenly left in an eerie silence that neither of us seemed to have the words to fill. On the night where we should have been at our closest, celebrating the start of our new life together, I had never felt further away from him, from everything. So, we did what we did best. Why talk about your problems, when you can drown them out instead? We got stoned, ordered pizza and had sex for the second time. It was just as terrible as the first time.

The next night, we opened the flood gates and let in the masses. Our housewarming party was always going to be the event of the year and it didn't disappoint. All of our friends were there and some of their friends too, but we were celebrating, so the more the merrier. People spilled out into the garden (our garden) and into the hallway (our hallway) and even into the street (our street). I had no idea we had so many people who cared this much about us that they wanted to celebrate our new lives with us, to be part of our lives still, even after leaving the old one behind. For those first few days, as our housewarming party slipped from Friday, into Saturday and then into Sunday, surrounded by people who cared about me, I felt for the first time in my life that I was free. I had left the shackles of angst and adolescence behind me and had become a carefree, grounded, normal adult. There were no monsters lurking in the shadows, no gaping holes waiting to swallow me up. I had succeeded in leaving all of that, and my old self behind. Now, I was a new person with not a care in the world. The new me loved this new life. Let the party go on forever.

A few days after we moved in, my dad called and asked if he could pick me up from the flat. Expecting that he had come to his senses and wanted to apologise and make amends, I agreed to meet with him. When I got into his car, I waited nervously for an apology to come. But instead, he pulled abruptly away from the curb back into the line of traffic without a thought, "Right then, I suppose you'll be expecting lunch then aye?"

I sat quietly as he forced small talk to cut through the silence between us. The more he spoke, the more I could feel my blood heat in my veins. Heat radiated from my skin, burning with rage from inside out. How could he be so cold? How could he expect me to forget that only 2 days ago, he tried to rip my world from under my feet? Jamie, still shaken from being torn apart, felt like every problem the world had ever faced was a result of his very being. That every breath he exhaled was filling the air with poison. How could he cause such pain on a person, and then talk to me about the weather and the inconvenience that newly erected road works had caused to his day?

After about 10 minutes of small talk and rising tension, I couldn't take it anymore. I asked him if he was planning to apologise at all.

"What exactly would I have to apologise for?" he demanded, his eyes glaring at me as we sat in traffic at a red light.

"What do mean, what do you have to apologise for? You were completely out of order the other day! I can't believe you could say all those things about Jamie! He was absolutely humiliated and so am I!" I felt adrenaline carry me through the moment, the first time I had ever stood up to my dad.

"THAT boy, came into our house and destroyed our family! Everything was fine before he arrived. And now, I've lost my wife because of him. The only thing that stopped me from kicking his good-for-nothing ass out of my house earlier was your mother. The only reason I haven't been able to tell him exactly what I think of him, was your mother. And now your mother's decided she cares more about that waste of space than me, I can say whatever I like."

I could see the pent-up rage that he'd held on to for the last year boiling over the surface. His eyes bulged; his jaw clenched. The veins in his neck were pulsating with red hot blood, causing his face to turn from pink to red. I had never seen him so angry. I had never felt so angry myself. My dad had always been so close minded and unreasonable, I'm not sure why I was even surprised.

"You're fucking delusional!" The first time I had ever intentionally sworn in front of either of my parents.

"What did you just say? Just because you've moved out doesn't mean to can speak to me however you want, young lady!"

"Actually, it does. If you can say all those things about Jamie that aren't even true, then I can say whatever the *fuck* I want to you. You blame him for breaking up your marriage? Did it ever occur to you that mum got sick of you because you're a total fuckin' asshole and actually, we were all happier whenever you weren't around! Mum's going to be better off without you and so will I!"

"Well, if you think you're better off without me, then I guess you won't need your monthly allowance, will you? Didn't think of that, did you, you little smartass? How are you going to pay the rent on your fancy new flat without my help, eh? Apologise to me this very second or you're on your own."

By now, the traffic light had changed to green and cars behind us were beeping their horns. But we didn't move, as my dad continued to stare me down, trying to intimidate me into thinking I needed him. I didn't need him, and I didn't need his abuse. And no amount of money in the world would be worth spending one more minute with that man. I didn't even give him a response. I walked out of his car that day and never looked back. I'd find a way to pay my rent cheque. Some things are more important than money.

*

A few months into our new flat and our housewarming party was still going on, and we were loving life. We were surrounded by friends who loved us. Friends who were happy to help us celebrate our new life and freedom round the clock.

It was a common scene each morning for the house to be scattered with lifeless bodies, one by one slowly coming back to this planet. It often took several hours of confused silence and painful groaning before conversation would start up again, *"I was so fuckin' wasted last night"*. It had become a running joke that our house didn't start each day with *'good morning'* but instead *'I was so fucking wasted last night'*, usually followed by a half-conscious chorus of *'yeah'*, because at this point, it was all most of us could manage.

One morning, or more likely, one early afternoon, before any first words had come to light, Ryan bolted awake as if he'd had a nightmare, looked around the half-conscious room and said with some amount of panic in his voice, "Shit man, I had a conversation with a fucking lamp post last night. For like an hour." He sat back, stunned at himself, at the drug-induced creativity of his own mind. The rest of us speechless at the sudden outburst of what most people would have seen as madness.

"I think, I got into a fight with a car," Jamie announced, holding up his hand, his knuckles bloody and raw from the memory of repeatedly punching an inanimate object.

Everyone had a crazy story of how they spent the night before. I remember clearly one night after acquiring some particularly potent supply, being privy to some very private conversations between the neighbourhood plant communities, broadcasts in fact. Often on an evening, a group of us would go on an 'adventure' to the shop at the end of the road. Our street was lined by terraced houses, fronted by small, compartmentalised gardens, separated by 3-foot-high hedges, standing protectively between each garden - *to keep in the secrets*. As I walked past the hedges which were shielding the community of plant life between them, I heard them. They didn't want me to, but I did, loud and clear. I heard them clearer than I could hear my own thoughts. As I walked down the street, I could hear the plants ahead of me conversing behind the hedges. Talking of current affairs, politics. They spoke as if they were guests being interviewed on a TV talk show. I heard them discussing camera angles and lighting, announcing the fact that they were ready to go live in *3, 2, 1*. But as I approached each hedge, all I heard was *'Shh! Someone's coming!'*. The spotlights went off and everything went silent. The plants went back to being plants. Every garden I passed, the same thing happened. At first, I was pretty freaked out. But by the time we reached the end of the road, I was crouching behind the hedges, eavesdropping on the secret lives of the talk show plants.

It wasn't long before it all came crashing down around me, when I saw Tom for the first time. I hadn't seen him since school ended and I knew he was avoiding me for the same reason I felt I had to avoid him. But it didn't make it hurt any less. And it didn't make me stop missing him. I always knew it was the way things had to be, but still I felt like part of me was missing. Jamie and I had a life together now, I knew I couldn't have them both, but it seemed the choice was made for me. I didn't even really get to say goodbye. Since I unexpectedly never made it to my last day of school, I didn't know that my second to last day of school, would in fact be my last. My last day of school, and my last day with Tom. I tried to remember the last thing I said to him, but I couldn't. It was nothing, because I didn't know that it needed to be anything, that I would want to remember it. It wasn't meant to end this way. It was meant to be everything. I pictured our goodbye like in the old movies. Fraught with such intensity that you could cut straight through the air from the other side of the screen. Desperate black and white lovers, breathless, painful at the thought of living without each other. Torrential rain drowning the scene in despair and heartache, soaking the pair to the bone. A terrible realisation that true love does not always avail. I pictured a movie goodbye with all the honesty and passion that I had been lacking from Tom (and myself), being unleashed in that one final moment, when finally, he realised that his time had run out. As we parted for the final time, I pleaded to him with my eyes not to let me go. I saw in his eyes his reply, that he couldn't, that our fate was already written. But as I reluctantly turned to walk away, he grabbed my wrist, hard, and hot with passion, his eyes wild with desperation burning right into my soul.

"Stay with me."

It's all he ever needed to say. Only he never said it, so I left.

Similarly, I imagined our reunion to be movielike. I spent hours imagining how he would burst through the front door, ignoring everything and everyone in his path. He would stretch out his hand to me, pulling me to my feet and into his arms.

"Come with me."

"I thought you'd never ask."

But actually, what happened is that he broke my heart.

He turned up unexpected as if he had been there a thousand times before, immediately blending into the crowd before I even realised he was in my house. I heard his laugh from the other room before I knew he was there. My stomach flipped, butterflies scrambling, desperately trying to break free. For what seemed like hours, I was rooted to the spot, terrified to find out if it was actually him, terrified at seeing him again after all this time apart. I was desperate to see him, but also so desperate not to have to. I was happy to stay, enjoying the sound of his laughter from afar, a laughter that I had missed so much. Ryan brought me out of my frozen state with a thud.

"Is that Tom?" he shouted at me excitedly.

He grabbed my hand and pulled me towards the sound of his voice. A few others followed and Tom was greeted like a celebrity. Once the crowd around him had died down, it was my turn. I moved towards him, waiting for his response, our big, emotional reunion. After a few seconds, our eyes met. It only took a second to see that they were no longer full of the love and care that I remember. They were cold and blank.

"Hey," he nodded to me as if I were a stranger.

There was no love. There was no hate. There was just, nothing.

And just as quickly, he melted back into the crowd. I felt myself crumple to the floor, a pool of blood gushing around me from where he had stabbed me straight through the heart.

The rest of the night was torture. Watching him laughing and joking with our friends, but not being able to go to him. I had grown pretty used to not getting what I wanted from Tom, but to be in the same room as him, to constantly catch his eye, to hear his voice, to know that he doesn't want me near him, I could hardly stand it. He was there for a party, and the fact that it was at my house, in my space, was irrelevant. *Is everyone else only here for the party?* He wasn't there for me. *Nobody is here for me.*

I spent the night miserable, trying my hardest to get drunk enough to no longer care. It didn't work. I had never been so glad to wake up the next morning, knowing that Tom wouldn't be there, that I wouldn't have to see him. He made his point. *"I don't need you"*. Like a knife, straight to the heart. Then I thought that I might never see him again, and that was even worse.

I felt flat. Like I had lost a part of myself, part of my soul. The Tom I knew and loved was well and truly gone. I had never been so surrounded by so many people in my life, yet, I had never felt so alone. *If I just disappeared, would anybody even notice? Nobody would notice.*

Chapter 11 – The Cost of Living

It didn't take long before Jamie and I realised that adult life came at a price. In between the endless parties, drugs and booze, there was rent to pay, and mouths to feed. And without a monthly allowance, it was a lot more difficult than we had anticipated.

We both managed to secure jobs at a nearby hotel, working the breakfast shift in the restaurant, serving 7 a.m. bacon and eggs. It seemed ideal. Starting early meant finishing early so we could still spend the majority of the day hanging out with our friends and going to work while they slept off the night before. But the work was hard and relentless, lack of sleep catching up with us as our late-night party lifestyle constantly clashed with early morning shifts. The money and the hours were poor.

I remember we were both so excited to go and pick up our first pay cheques. The last of my allowance had run out long ago. It had helped cover the first month's rent and bills, but by this point, we had been without any 'spending money' for several weeks now. We walked quickly to work to pick up our first square brown envelope, freedom and endless possibility sealed inside. We talked excitedly of how we were going to spend it. We would go on our first ever shopping trip together to *Iceland*, just like a normal couple. We would buy burgers and oven chips, ice-cream and strawberry sauce, a massive multipack of crisps to share out between our friends, waffles, mini-pizzas, chocolate bars, a cake from the bakery to celebrate. We would have to get a taxi home after buying so much food that we wouldn't be able to carry it home. But that's OK, we'd been paid, so we could afford it. Later that night, we would go out for the first time since living in the city. Every week we stayed at home while our friends went out to bars or to gigs. But we had never been able to scrimp together the £10 for us both to get in, so we stayed home and waited for them to come to ours afterwards, where they could tell us in grave detail, everything we had missed. But this week, we would go with them. We would even go out for dinner on the way, *Sizzlers,* the best dirty burgers in town! It would be our first date night since leaving home. I felt butterflies flutter in my gut at the thought of going on a date with the man I loved, it was just what we needed, some alone time.

When we arrived at the hotel, our pay packets were waiting patiently for us behind the reception desk. We ripped them open the minute they touched our hands, like eager children on Christmas morning. I held out my hand and let the contents of the envelope slide out into my hand. *Wow, real money.* Suddenly all the hard hours and early mornings were worth it.

After we left the hotel, richer than we had ever been in our lives, we found a quiet spot in a nearby park where we could work out our finances. It was our first month living as adults and we were determined to do it responsibly. We would need to put some aside for the rent cheque at the end of the month, some for the electric meter, and the rest would be ours. I felt our hopes and dreams for the next 2 weeks come crashing down around us as we realised what we had left. We were left with less than £50 between us. Less than an hour after receiving our first pay cheque and we were already counting down to the next, in 2 weeks' time.

Our trip to Iceland was not as much fun as we thought it would be. There was no ice-cream or strawberry sauce, no waffles, no mini-pizzas, just essentials to get us through the next 2 weeks. Everything was so expensive. We opted for rice, pasta, beans, chicken nuggets, anything cheap that we thought we could stretch as far as we could.

We knew already that the food we bought wouldn't last the whole 2 weeks. Just like we had been doing for the last month, we would have to rely on the generosity of our friends. Our friends were using our flat as a free-for-all party zone, but they always brought food, for when the munchies kick in. There were always *Rustler* burgers, micro-chips and super noodles piled up high in the kitchen for midnight snacks. We would just have to survive on that for our evening meals. We were lucky also to be working in a restaurant. There was always a big breakfast guaranteed at the end of a shift. So even if we couldn't afford any food at all, at least we would always get breakfast.

There was no taxi home. We walked home, stopping every few minutes to rest our arms every time we thought they might drop off. And we would miss out on yet another gig night. But nothing could stop us going on our well-needed date night. We decided to save £10 of our money so we could still go to Sizzlers.

That night we took all the money we had in the world and spent it on burgers and chips, and it felt like the best decision we had ever made. We deliberated for at least 10 minutes at the counter, letting the other customers skip while we took our time deciding on the perfect burger combos to get. We both knew that it might be a while before we got another treat like this, so it had to be just right. I opted for Sizzlers' signature burger with chilli and cheese, and Jamie went for the old classic, cheese and bacon. We waited anxiously as the burgers were prepared, but it felt like hours. I had never been so excited about a burger before. When they came, we sat in silence, enjoying the burgers more than each other. It was the best thing I had ever eaten in my life. It was ecstasy. For a few minutes while I enjoyed the taste of the greasy, salty, spicy beef in my mouth and belly, I was in heaven. It had only been a little over a month since we left home, but already it felt like so long since we had had any luxury, but it wasn't until that night that we realised what we had been missing. We had been living in depravity, and getting that slight glimpse of what we were missing out on, was only going to make it harder to live without. But for that moment, I had my chilli burger, and that's all that mattered.

Afterwards we walked to *Lava*, where our friends had been that night to see a band play, just in time to meet the excited crowds spilling out onto the pavements in front of the club. Everyone had been raving about seeing the band tonight and we were already dreading hearing about how amazing they were and how we 'should have been there'. Out of all of our friends, we were the only ones living independently, and the only ones with rent to pay. None of them understood that it was not out of choice that we were missing out on these things. And none of them understood how much it hurt to see everyone around us enjoy the things we knew we couldn't. I never told anyone about the pleasure I experienced devouring that burger, they wouldn't have understood anyway.

When our friends managed to comb their way through the crowd to meet us on the edge of it, it was just as we expected. *"Oh my god that was EPIC!" "That was THE BEST GIG EVER!" You need to start coming to more gigs, man, you're missing out some awesome music!"* I felt Jamie grip my hand tighter, he was feeling the same pain of missing out as I was.

When the band emerged onto the street behind the crowd, they were instantly surrounded by fans asking for autographs. Our own friends scattered too, but we hung back and waited, how could we go and speak to a band that we didn't actually go to see? *"I never went to your gig because I couldn't afford a ticket. But I heard you rocked it"*. Instead, we stood at the other side of the street waiting for people to be ready to leave and walk back to the/our flat, missing out once again. Just then, Ryan, who had been over talking to the band with everyone else, came running over.

"They invited us to get pizza with them! Just see you at the party later, yeah?!"

He screamed back to them like a little girl who had just met her pop idol, and they disappeared into the next-door kebab shop. I couldn't understand what the big deal was. They went to gigs every weekend and never had I seen anyone ask for an autograph or seen Ryan scream like a girl over anyone. Most of the bands that played were kids that we knew from school and other locals, and they didn't get reactions like this. The following weekend I was at my mum's house for a hot meal and an MTV fix, and there they were. As if that night didn't cause enough regret, that band later turned out to be one of my favourite bands for many years to come. I spent a long time livid that I had missed out. I missed the gig, I missed meeting them, eating pizza with them. Until one day, the singer was arrested for child molesting and his involvement in a paedophilia ring. I guess sometimes things do work out for the best, even if it doesn't seem that way at the time.

Chapter 12 – The Day the World Ended

I remember the day the world changed. Like it was yesterday.

I had spent the last few months living inside a bubble. Safe in the knowledge that my incapacitated state-of-mind would cushion my fall and protect me from any more blows the world decided to send my way. I couldn't take any more blows. But the thing about bubbles is, they burst. And one day, it did. And all the toxins and sharp edges of this serrated world that I had so desperately tried to shield myself from, all hit me at once. All I could do was watch, as everything crumbled, and come crashing down around me. Literally.

The morning it happened, Jamie and I were working in the hotel. We had finished our breakfast shift already, but Jamie had managed to get a few extra hours in the laundry room. Since he couldn't leave until everything was done, I had secretly been helping him get through his work faster so that we could both leave earlier. I liked the laundry room. Upstairs in the restaurant, it was loud and full of people. We were, of course, expected to be pleasant to hotel guests at all times, (which was exhausting), even when they were not pleasant in return (which was infuriating). But in the laundry room, it was just us. There were no arrogant businessmen demanding to know why their breakfast was taking so long. No self-important managers complaining that my tie was done up wrong or my skirt was too short. There was no noise and no distraction. Just Jamie. We'd been working as a team all week, and by now had quite an efficient system to get through all the piles of laundry quickly, without confusing which is clean and which is dirty (which is harder than you would think). I felt like we were back to our old selves again, the way we used to be when we first met. The way we were when we couldn't stand to be apart, when every moment without him was torture. Before we became the couple who had nothing left to say to one another. The couple who grew awkward, when there was no one around to mediate the conversation between us. Jamie and I had grown so used to spending all our time in a crowd, that we had forgotten how to be couple. I couldn't remember the last time we spent this much time alone. We laughed all week. Playing about and having fun together. We acted young and carefree, just like how we were supposed to be. This is how our life together was meant to be. And I felt like it was finally starting. I was starting to remember that I *chose* to be here, to be with him. And there's nowhere that I'd have rather been, and no one I'd rather be with.

That morning, I was happily sorting sheets into piles, while Jamie delivered the fresh clean sheets to the cleaners' cupboards on each floor of the hotel. Suddenly, he rushed in, out of breath with madness in his eyes.

"World war fucking three just started!" he gushed.

Every morsel fear I had ever felt, all rushed to the pit of my stomach, nearly knocking me off my feet. I felt bile rush up my throat, threatening to further dirty the sheets that now lay pooled and forgotten at my feet. I didn't need to hear any more. I always knew one day that the world would end. I guess *this*, was that day.

"Don't be ridiculous! You're so melodramatic!" I tried to laugh it off.

"No. I'm serious. Come see."

He held his hand out, reaching for mine. His face was like stone.

I reached for his hand, but my feet didn't move. He pulled me from the spot, his wild eyes never leaving mine. He pulled me all through the corridors of the basement of the hotel, up the stairs into the hotel bar, and into a crowd of people. I still had no idea what was going on. I looked around the crowd at the stunned faces. Some with their hands over their mouths, some holding their heads in their hands. People were crying, hugging into the safety of the person next to them. The scene before me played out in slow motion. The sound went out. I could hear my own heartbeat, pounding hard, trying to keep the blood circulating in my frozen body. *This is it.*

"What's going on?" I asked aimlessly to the crowd of people.

Nobody answered. Did I say that out loud? Jamie's glazed expression blended into the rest of the crowd and I felt like I was the only one left on this planet. Nobody spoke. It was as if the world was on mute. Panicked by the silence, my heart beat louder. Then I realised that the crowd was gathered around a TV screen anchored to the ceiling. I turned my attention to the screen. The shots moved between images of thick black smoke, to crowds on a street, where everyone had the same alienated expression as the people around me. *What the fuck is going on?!* I had never seen a crowd react like this. I could see from the screen that there had been an explosion of some kind, but it was nothing that didn't happen every day all over the world. But immediately, this felt different. This felt like the whole world had just, stopped.

Suddenly, the crowd around me gasped in terror. I looked up at the screen just in time to see a jumbo jet fly straight into the side of a skyscraper. Live. I tried to tell myself that we were watching some Hollywood disaster movie. But the fear in the air around me told me it wasn't true, that what we were seeing was no movie, it was real. I felt my stomach twist painfully into shapes I'd never experienced before. My legs buckled and I fell backwards as if I'd been punched in the stomach. Jamie stood behind me as if anticipating my defeat. He caught me and held me tight, the only thing stopping me from dissipating into the air around. I gasped for breath, but the air stuck in my throat as my thoughts suffocated me. '*This is it. This is how the world will end. This is how I'm going to die. This is how we're all going to die*'.

My mind was a swirl of terror. My dreams, plagued by deafening explosions, blasts so close that afterwards, the air is muffled and silent. I heard screams, real screams of real terror from people that I had never met before. I woke up, gasping for air, fighting to get out of the thick cloud of smoke. I never realised that something that happened so far away, to strangers that I had no feelings for, could resonate so clearly on the other side of the world. But it wasn't just me that felt that way. You could feel it in the air as you walked down the street. The air was heavy, laden with fear. It was a whole new world.

All week I kept hearing *"My cousin lives in New York; we're so relieved she's OK", "My dad just flew home from the states the day before, it could have been him"*. It could have been anyone. It could have been me. I couldn't stop thinking about all those cousins in New York. The ones who were not OK. Even the ones who were OK, having to live with something so terrible right on their doorstep, having to walk past the aftermath every day.

On the news, they called it a terrorist attack. I had never heard the term terrorist attack before that day, no one had. The only times I've ever heard of such genocide, was in war. Something that happened far enough away that we could all lower our eyes in denial and get on with our days. But nobody could deny this. Nobody could look away from the horror that happened in *our* world, right on our doorstep. But a war was exactly what it turned out to be. Jamie wasn't wrong when he announced the beginning of world war three, only instead, they called the *'war on terror'*. Another new term that our whole generation learnt overnight.

I felt like nowhere was safe. I heard people talking about how Aberdeen could be the next target. The oil capital of Europe. Or London, with its tubes packed full of commuters. Or Edinburgh, with its millions of tourists coming from all over the world. It could happen anywhere, at any time. The hotel that Jamie and I worked in was in Aberdeen city center. Could we be a target? I thought of that every single day I worked there. I always knew that I sounded paranoid, but tell me, in a world where 200,000 people can die so tragically, just because they turned up for work on time last Tuesday morning, where is it that paranoia ends, and real-life threat begins?

All week I had been hearing about Nostradamus' theory; a French philosopher who predicted that two birds would fly into two towers, then the world would fall silent. He predicted that during the silence, the world would end. People laughed it off, calling him crazy. For the first part of his theory, he had been correct. And as for the second, I had always known the day would come when the world would end. It was simply a question of when. And as predicted, a few days after the towers fell, the world, for three long minutes, fell silent. And together, in silence, we waited for the beginning of the end of the world. People said it was crazy. But all I felt was fear. What if, during those three minutes, when the whole world has come together, and holds hands united, everything just, stops? What if it's not crazy? What if *I'm* not crazy? What if *I'm* the one who's been right all along?

That night, anticipating what may, or may not be our last night on earth, Jamie and I spent it together. I was surprised that he agreed to it. I expected him to laugh in my face and tell me I was paranoid and to get a grip. But he didn't. Instead, he banned everyone from the flat for the night so that we could spend the night alone.

Obviously, the world did not end. But to have an entire night alone with Jamie, in our own house, it almost would have been worth it. That night, he wasn't the cold, distant person that I'd been living with for the last few months. He wasn't the stranger that I could no longer talk to. He was the boy I fell in love with. He lit candles all over the flat, and he made us a beautiful dinner. For the first time in months, not only was he the boy that I had forgotten I was in love with, but he was the boy that I had forgotten was in love with me. We spent the night just being together, like couples are meant to. For hours, we lay in bed, safe in each other's arms, like there was no one else in the world but us. And if the world really had crumpled around our feet, I doubt we'd have even noticed.

Chapter 13 – Down the Rabbit Hole

A few months into my new life, and I was struggling to keep a hold of my own mind. My thoughts were no longer my own. Entwined with drug-induced illusions and paranoia, I could feel myself slipping away. Dizzy and disorientated, like Alice falling down the rabbit hole, deeper and deeper into an abyss. Just like the darkness that had been shadowing me for so many years, now too was my own lifestyle. This new world I was living in, it wasn't supporting me the way it should, it was destroying me. My thoughts, my life, my person, it was all gone, and now I was hollow. Swallowed up by a shallow lifestyle of binge drinking, drugs and parties, until there was nothing left. I had spent my first six months as an adult so consumed with getting lost, that I no longer knew my way back. I hadn't even noticed, until it was already too late. And then one day, I realised. It was like waking up from a terrible nightmare, only to realise that real life, the life that I had created for myself, was just as bad as everything I had tried so hard to drown out. It wasn't just me that was lost, everything was lost. I barely recognised myself. I looked around me and I barely recognised my own surroundings. I knew then that it was my own fault that things had gone so far. I should have noticed my own life getting out of control, but I couldn't see it. I should have pulled myself back before falling too far down the rabbit hole, but I didn't want to. I just let myself keep falling, over and over. In the beginning, I wanted to be lost, to come to a place so far away, that the darkness couldn't follow me. Only it didn't work, it did follow me, and now it was even darker. I thought when we left home, once we got far away, that things would somehow be different, that the world would be safe again. I thought I could leave my old life, my old, damaged self behind, but instead, I packed everything up and took it all with me. Now I felt even further away from home and I was still in darkness. Only now, I was alone.

The people I surrounded myself with, the ones I once called my friends, they were not friends, they were strangers. Friends that I have known for years, barely recognisable to me now, even Jamie. I missed him the most. He followed me into this world for the very same reasons, to distance himself from the rest of the world. He let himself drift away the same way that I did. We were meant to drift together. But instead, we only drifted further apart. By then, I felt further from him than I did from anything or anyone else. I felt like it was my fault. I led him there, he was lost too, because of me. He became, along with everyone else I thought I knew, someone I didn't even recognise. The drugs changed him. The kind and sweet and gentle person that I fell in love with, he was gone now. Now, instead of the perfect new life together that I had once imagined, we simply existed together, lost down the rabbit-hole, never able to find each other. By then, I was so lost myself that I didn't see that he was lost too. He was a shell of the boy I once knew. And although he no longer talked to me the way he used to, the way he used to tell me everything, I knew anyway that he was plagued with shadows, just like I was. I knew he couldn't see any more clearly than I could. Jamie was a new person now. He was angry and vicious, and I couldn't stand to be around him. The feeling was mutual. I knew he didn't want me around. It was sad that it had come to this, with so much hatred between us. It was only a year since we first met, from when I thought he would be my prince charming, whisking me away to a far-off land where we would live happily ever after. That was the plan. But now we were so far away from that, it seemed impossible to go back. The only way was down, and Jamie was falling just as fast as I was.

But what about everybody else? The ones I called my friends, could they see this downward spiral that I was on? Did they see, but just not care enough to pull me out before everything was gone? I could see them functioning in their normal lives, as they flit in and out of mine. I had become nothing more than simply part of the social circus that they amuse themselves with for a night or two before returning back to the normal world, a world that I had long since left behind. I started to doubt that I had any real friends left in the world. That familiar voice whispering in my ear again '*If you were gone, nobody would even miss you*'.

I remember clearly, the moment I finally saw through the haze and realised that this was happening, that I had completely lost control. In our house, every day was a party. It started off with just our group of friends from school, who would come and stay with us at the weekends. We were the only ones in our group to live without parents, so it was a 'free-house' every night. It was a novelty for everyone, including us. In the beginning, it was so great to have people around us all the time. I loved the idea that people came to spend time with us. I realised now that it was never us they came to see. They just came for a place to hang out, where they could get wasted without worrying about getting caught.

As time went on, the group got bigger, the parties more out of control, until we were in business seven nights a week. A lot of our original friends have already gone, sick of our new party lifestyle and too busy getting on with their own lives. At the end of the summer, most of them went off to university or got *real* jobs, some back to school, back to real life, where they didn't need us anymore. Now, it was *friends* of friends that filled our house, and friends of *their* friends, to the point where I didn't even know most of them. One night, I came home from work to a house full of people; a usually welcomed situation. Only, when I looked around the crowd of people, there was not one person I recognised, not even Jamie. How did all these people come to be in my house? Had they been here all along? Had I been so wasted all these months that I never noticed my own house filling with strangers? As I stood in the doorway to what was suddenly a very unfamiliar scene, I watched a girl, thoughtlessly flicking her cigarette ash onto the carpet, *my* carpet, as she talked and laughed with her friends. I pushed my way through the crowd to her.

"What the fuck do you think you're doing?" I demanded, gesturing at her cigarette. "And who the fuck *are* you anyway?"

She stood, mouth gaping at me, stunned that I could be so rude to burst into her conversation. She spun around to face me head on. She looked me up and down in disgust for several seconds before turning to laugh with her friend. Just as I was growing more and more ready to personally pick her scrawny body up and throw her out the window, she decided to grace me with a response.

"I'm *Jan*. Who the fuck are *you*?"

I stood, shocked. How dare this little bitch talk to me like that in my own house!? Hot blood raced through me and I was just about to launch myself at her full force, when Jamie bounded over and pushed me back into the other room before I got a chance to protest.

"What the fuck are you doing? Did you not hear what that little bitch said to me? What the fuck is she doing here anyway? I've never even seen her before!"

Jamie shrugged.

"So? It's a fuckin party, chill out, man!" and he leaped away, back into the sea of strangers.

Wasn't this his house too? How could he not care that people were trashing our house? People we didn't even know.

For the first time in six months, I took a look around the flat and saw all the damage that had been left behind after the world's longest party. There were holes in the walls where people had punched their way through the plasterboard. There was graffiti and huge sections of bare wall where the wallpaper had been ripped down. The carpet was soiled with burns and stains, only covered up by the littering of beer cans and cigarette butts that people had tossed away. The lock had been ripped off the bathroom door, the toilet seat sat detached and broken next to the bowl which, much like the walls around it, was streaked with old vomit. How could I let it get this way? This was my home, and I was the one who let this happen.

The following day while Jamie was at work, I threw everyone out and spent the whole day cleaning the flat from top to bottom, trying to return it back to a liveable state, the way it was when we first moved in. The flat wasn't anything special. But the carpets weren't burnt, and the walls didn't have holes in them, and it was ours. I decided, as of that day, that the party was over. After I finished, I sat, content in our clean, unusually quiet house, and waited for Jamie to get back form work. I knew we had to talk, to get things back on track. But we had been so in sync with one another once before, and I knew that we could get things back to the way they were meant to be. Things hadn't been good between us for a while, but I had never given up hope that one day, they could be again. We just needed to take back control. Put a stop to the drugs and the parties, and then everything would be ok.

But once again, I had it all wrong. Jamie didn't want to hear it. I spent all day cleaning the house from top to bottom, trying to make it back into the home that it was meant to be for us. I spent the last of our money for that week on fresh food so that I could make dinner for us, so that it would be waiting for him when he came home from work. I wanted so desperately to show him how it could be. How it would be, if it was just us again. I wanted to show him that we could still be in love, if we wanted to be. I wanted to show him how it was meant to be. All those times that we sat in my room at my mum's house, imagining how perfect our lives would be once we left. We would be so happy together. We would be free. And we still could be, couldn't we?

But that night Jamie never came home from work. All night I waited, alone. I let the dinner go cold and dry, the candles I lit burnt out, but he never came. One by one, uninvited guests filled their usual spaces, oblivious to the household that was torn apart without anyone even noticing. If a tree falls in the forest but no one is around to hear it, does it make a sound?

Jamie stumbled home around 2 a.m., just in time for the height of the party. He staggered past me, tripping over his own feet and falling face first into our bed without so much as greeting me.

The next morning, I tried again to talk to him. I asked him patiently why he didn't come home from work last night. I told him that I had cleaned and that I made him dinner. I told him that I wanted to talk about us. I told him that I missed him. Before I could even explain myself properly, he went berserk. He jumped up out of bed like a wild animal, shouting that he had had enough of my drama. That my misery was dragging him and everyone else around me down.

"You're killin' my fuckin' buzz, man. Get over yourself."

He called me a crazy bitch, that he was sick of all my fucking drama and so was everyone else. That all I ever do is nag him. That he was done with me.

He rounded up the sleeping bodies in the other room and led them out of the flat, promising them a "fuckin' bender". Nobody refused. Before I knew it, I was alone again. But wasn't I always? I felt the pit of my stomach sharpen as I realised that no matter how much I tried to change my life, I would always end up this way, wishing I was somewhere else, and wondering why I was even bothering to try.

I sat for a while in the empty flat that managed to stay clean for a single day and was now trashed again. I couldn't stand to stay there for another minute. I took myself out, hoping that the fresh air would stop my head from spinning.

I found myself in a park, with no plan and no intention of making one. I just wanted to be somewhere else for a while. I was surrounded by people, living their lives. Parents playing with their children, a group of sunny pre-teens playing frisbee. Couples engrossed in each other, picnicking with scotch eggs and cheap wine. Everyone around me seemed so ignorantly content. Why were *they* not having to force themselves to take each next breath? Why were *they* not so full of hate, the way that I was? Certainly, none of *them* seemed like crazy bitches who drive everyone else around them mad. My mind raced with poisonous thoughts as I recycled all the words that Jamie threw at me earlier. *Maybe he's right. Maybe I am a crazy bitch. Maybe they're all better off without me. You've always known that!* I suddenly became overcome with fatigue, exhausted from always wanting something more, but never getting it. I just wanted everything to stop. I wanted to feel nothing. Surrounded by all the sharp reminders of all the things I knew I'd never have, I cut myself so badly that Jamie, when he found me later, called an ambulance.

This time I cut my wrists, and I meant it. I wanted so badly to have the courage to press harder, to cut deeper, but I couldn't do it, another failure. I was in A & E for less time than it took for the ambulance to drive me there. They bandaged me up and sent me on my way, leaving Jamie and I to walk the 4 miles home without so much as a second thought. I couldn't even get that right. Now all I was left with were some bright new scars and a boyfriend who resented me more than ever. The next morning, he acted as if nothing had happened, just like he had been doing since the day we moved in.

We spent the next few weeks pretending that each other didn't exist. By then, my scars had almost healed, but then all the reasons they happened in the first place were still the same. The parties continued, Jamie actively encouraging them. I started to worry that sometimes he didn't even know I was still around. And after finding him with another girl in our own house, while I was in the next room, I knew my worries were real. I knew then, that if I left, he wouldn't even notice I was gone.

I just couldn't stand to be there anymore. My mind kept circling back to the day in the park, if only I had been stronger, if only I'd had the courage to go deeper, I would be gone from here. I had tried so hard to keep afloat, but I was drifting further and further out to sea like I was caught in a current, I was drowning. My first thought was to kill myself, to try again to be stronger. I felt like I was fighting a battle that I couldn't possibly win, so why bother? My second thought was my mother. Needless to say, I chose the latter. I called my mum and told her I wanted to go home. Within 30 minutes, she was there, holding me and telling me that everything will be OK.

Chapter 14 - Home Alone

The day I moved home to my mum's house, I left them all. Every friend I had in the world, I left them all back at the flat with Jamie. I needed to leave them behind in my old life, in order to have a chance of a new one. It took Jamie 2 days to realise I was gone. I sat breathless for 2 days, waiting for my phone to finally ring. Part of me wished he would call, begging forgiveness for not trying harder to save us. He would cry and promise me that we would be OK, if I came home to him where I belonged, the way things were meant to be. But he didn't cry or beg, he shouted and swore and promised that one day I would get everything that was coming to me for leaving him to pay the rent on his own. As for everyone else that I left behind, that's where they stayed, I hardly heard from any of them again, including Ryan, who I had been friends with since we were kids, and who was suddenly a friend of Jamie's, rather than a friend of mine. I didn't blame them; I could only imagine what awful things Jamie was telling them all, now that I wasn't there to defend myself. He said he would make me regret leaving, presumably by ensuring that I could never return to it, even if I wanted to. Part of me thought "let him say what he likes, I don't need them". I felt freer than I ever had before. All they ever did was hold me back, I didn't need them, I didn't want them. But the other part of me felt like I had been beaten to within an inch of my life.

Now that I was truly on my own, I felt lonelier than ever. At least now it was quiet. Everything was so noisy before; I couldn't even tell what was real. It was like an untuned TV, so full of static that, although you know there's still a picture underneath, you can't quite make out what it is. But now there was no static, only quiet. Silence. Now that it was so quiet, I could hear the real noise. I'd been trying to block it for so long, but now that I was finally letting it be heard, I felt like it was screaming at me. All the noise that had been blocked for the last year, all screaming at once. If you lock up a wild animal in a soundproof room, walked away and ignored it for a year, how much angrier do you imagine it will be when you finally let it out?

I felt like my whole life had been snatched away from me. Everyone in my life that was close to me was gone. After weeks of radio silence from my so-called friends, I realised that I had been wrong about so many things. Were any of them ever really friends? Did anyone ever really care? All the demons whispering in my ear all these years, they had been right all along. *'No one cares about you. No one will even notice you're gone. They are better off without you'.* It's like everything I thought I knew had been swept away, and all that was left, was me. Jamie, on the other hand, I couldn't seem to get away from. For weeks he plagued me with angry, threatening texts and phone calls, constant reminders of what a heartless bitch I was. It amazed me that someone who once loved me to the end of the earth, could hold so much hatred for me now.

After I moved back home, my mum quickly became my best friend. Every single one of my friends had let me down, but my mum never had, and I knew she never would. I felt guilty for not realising sooner, that all the times I thought I was completely on my own, I never was. I had even managed to strike a truce with my brother. After the hell of the last few months, the brother that I had spent my life fighting and bickering with, suddenly didn't seem so bad. Now that Dad was gone, it was just the three of us, and it felt like this was how it was always meant to be. It was like we were an entirely differently family; a happy one. The atmosphere at home was so much more relaxed, like the air was somehow lighter, and for the first time ever, we were all enjoying spending time as a family.

And just like any other family home, there were always chores to do. But after being responsible for my own home for the last six months, they no longer seemed so bad. And now that Dylan and I seemed to be on the same team, we usually found a way of making them a bit more enjoyable. One weekend, mum asked us both to dismantle an old armchair, so that she could fit it in her car to take it to the skip. *"Dismantle the chair so it fits in the car"* were the only instructions left, further interpretation of those instructions was up to us. Then she went off to work and left us to it. So, *how are we going to do this?* we thought. We sat over breakfast, maturely discussing what would be the most efficient way to carry out our mission. In the end, we decided that the best way to achieve *"dismantle the chair so it fits in the car"* was to smash it to pieces, agreeing that this would both *"dismantle the chair"* and allow it to *"fit in the car"*. I must admit, seeing it written down in front of me now, it does seem like quite a destructive way to go about things. But it seemed like the perfect solution at the time.

Dylan and I hauled the oversized armchair into the back garden and into the middle of the lawn. After hunting through the shed for some suitable smashing tools, all we could find was 2 garden spades. *That'll do the trick!* we thought. So, while I checked the garden to make sure there were no pets lurking nearby that might get smashed in the process, Dylan prepared some appropriate music...*Rage Against the Machine*...what else? Ready for smashing, we surrounded the chair, lifting our spades above our heads, preparing for the first blow.

"Let's do this," I announced, eager to smash something innocent to pieces - just what I needed.

"No, wait!" Dylan shouted.

He lifted his spade into position over his shoulder and waited. "Just wait."

It took me a second to realise what he was waiting for. The intro to *Bomb Track* played through his bedroom window, building up tension to when the song explodes into angry guitars and, well, rage. We waited. Anticipation built as the intro grew heavier and faster, closing in on the explosion. As I waited, I let my head fill with every shit thing that anyone had ever done to me. Every person who has ever crossed me, everyone who had ever cheated me or stabbed me in the back. I thought about Jamie, about Tom, Ryan, Becca, Hannah, myself. I stared into the leather of the chair and saw the faces of everyone who put me in this place I was in now; alone and broken and having to fight to keep myself standing. All I wanted to do was break them, the way they broke me. I don't know what flooded Dylan's mind as he waited to smash the shit out of that chair, but I could see in his eyes that something did.

Then finally, BOOM! Our spades crashed down into the chair, just in time to celebrate the explosion of drums and metal guitars ripping through the air. Both spades hit so hard that they bounced halfway back through the air. I heard the wooden frame snapping beneath the leather.

We hit again and again until we were out of breath. I stood back, catching my breath. I was enraged. I felt like my whole body was on fire, rage screaming out of me after years of oppression. I felt like I had been held under water, drowning and finally, I had surfaced, gasping for air and fighting for my life. If I had known how amazing it felt to smash the shit out of things, I would have tried it sooner! Eventually, we both ran out of steam; emotionally and physically shattered.

As it turns out, spades do not smash through leather. And although we had done a pretty good job of breaking up the frame inside it, the chair was still in one piece and we had to cut the leather off to take it apart. As we sliced through the leather of the seemingly undamaged chair, millions of shattered pieces of wood spilled onto the grass. The leather exterior may have held the chair together, but inside, it was broken beyond repair. We began clearing the broken pieces into a pile in the driveway, mindfully placed to make it easier to move the now dismantled chair into the car; mission accomplished. However, once we had cleared away all the big pieces, we found that we were left with a new problem; the grass was now covered in shards of broken wood that were too small to pick up by hand. And since we couldn't let the dog back out into the garden until it was safe for him to walk on the grass, we had to find a way to clean it up. So, we had another strategic discussion about how best to solve our new problem. We couldn't pick up all the bits because they were too small and mostly embedded into the grass. We concluded that the only way to get up all the bits safely, was to hoover it, so that's what we did. At the time, it seemed like the only logical solution.

Now everything was cleaned up nicely, we sat down to a well-deserved wine/cider and waited for Mum to come through the door singing our praises. Eventually we heard the door go - Mum home from work.

"What, what is this?" we heard from the hallway.

Dylan and I looked at each other, confused. This did not sound like a mother singing praises. Instead, it was a tone which we were a little more familiar with - frustration and disappointment. She was still standing in doorway; she seemed shocked and confused.

"We dismantled the chair."

"You told us to."

Brothers in arms.

"I see that. But what have you done to my hoover?!"

"Oh. Well, we needed to clean up after. Sorry, I'll put it away now."

I'd never seen her so upset because we forgot to put the hoover away, but I honestly couldn't think what else she could be upset about. She told us to dismantle the chair, so we dismantled the chair. We even made sure we had cleaned up after ourselves.

"It's full of grass!"

Her face got redder and redder, a mixture of rage and confusion. It may not have been the most conventional use for a hoover, but there really was no other way - we discussed it.

"Well, we had to hoover up all the little bits of wood so we could let the dog out and they were too small to pick up."

My mum started to spin. She reminded me of one of those spinning tops that eventually just spun right up into the air.

"Where was the wood?"

"On the grass."

I was really missing the point by now. We had already established that the hoover was full of grass, hadn't we?

"So, you hoovered the grass?!"

"Well. Yes. But we needed to pick up the bits of wood."

What part did she not understand?

"So, you used my Dyson?! Do you have any idea how much those cost?"

Silence.

"Oh my God! Did anyone see you?"

What the fuck does that matter?!

"Probably. I think the guy over the fence was out at one point."

My mum was holding her head in her hands - probably to stop it from spinning away. She didn't speak to us for the rest of the night. And then spent the next month refusing to let us forget that we had gone out into the garden to hoover the grass with her Dyson. It seemed like the logical thing to do at the time, but now as a Dyson-owning adult myself, I have to admit that she had a point!

Chapter 15 - He Loves Me, He Loves Me Not

Now that I was back at my mum's house, I knew I had to move forward. I found that there *was* still some life out there, if you looked for it. In the six months I was away, a lot had changed. Everyone was now online, making it far easier to find new, or old friends to connect with, and I started chatting to a few new people that I knew from school. The anonymity of chatting online gave me a new sense of freedom to be who I wanted to be, instead of trying to fit into what everyone else around me was doing. It gave me the confidence to say what I was really feeling, without feeling like I would be judged.

I found a new confidant in Garry, an old friend from school that I hadn't spoken to since leaving. I told Garry things that I had never told anyone before. For the first time in my life, I felt safe enough to tell someone what I was really feeling. Talking to him online made me feel like I could say anything. Although he could read what I'd typed, he couldn't *see* me type it. It's anonymous. There's a kind of safety behind chatting online. Almost like you're not chatting to a real person, just to a text box on a screen. He could have been anyone, a total stranger, so I felt like I could tell him anything, and he wouldn't hold it against me.

I was finding it hard being back home and having someone to talk to, helped remind me that I wasn't as alone as I sometimes felt. Everything around me reminded me of how things used to be, before I left. At the time, I thought that everything was so dark, and I would have done anything to get out. But it didn't even compare to the black hole I fell into at the flat, and now, I would give anything to go back to the way things were before.

Amazingly, I found myself missing my old life.

Being back home again surrounded by constant reminders of my old life, I found myself thinking again about Tom. Everything reminded me of him. Now that my thoughts were no longer clouded, I missed him more than ever. I wondered if he still thought about me, did he miss me too? I wanted so much to find a way to get back there. For another chance with Tom, another chance at a new life. But after so long apart, I didn't know how to reach out to him. But I couldn't hold in my feelings anymore, I had to tell someone. And for the first time ever, after over a year of not having anyone to confide in, I told somebody how I felt about Tom.

I confided in Garry and he comforted me, reassuring me that Tom was missing me as much as I was missing him. He encouraged me to tell Tom how I felt. That now things were different, we could be different too. The thought of confronting Tom made me sick to my stomach. I couldn't shake the way he looked at me the last time I had seen him at the flat, like there was nothing left. I convinced myself that I was the last person on earth that he would ever want to see again, and I couldn't blame him.

One night, Garry came to meet me online as usual. But rather than the usual 'hello, how was your day?' Garry, in his excitement, skipped past all the pleasantries and went straight to the point.

Garry84 has just signed in.

Garry84 says: Saturday

Garry84 says: We're going to see Lord of the Rings

Gillibean says: Hello 2 u 2! lol

Garry84 says: Hi. On Saturday, we're all going 2C LOTR. It's gonna be shithot :D

Gillibean says: Lol. OK cool, sounds good.

…

Gillibean says: Who's we???

…Garry84 is typing a message…

Garry84 says: Me, u, Scotty & Tom

Garry84 says: ;)

(Insert long and painful internet silence here)

Gillibean says: I don't think he'll want 2 go if he knows I'm going

(Insert even longer internet silence and slight panic attack)

…Garry84 is typing a message…

Garry84 says: He knows, it's cool ;)

Garry84 says: Gotta go, IM me later!

Garry84 is signed off.

'It's cool'. *What the fuck does that mean?*

My heart sank into my stomach as I went into a mild state of panic.

I sat at that computer chair, staring at the empty chat for what felt like an hour, picking apart every syllable. 'It's cool'. *What the hell does that mean? Does that mean he wants to see me? Does he care so little about me that he's totally indifferent as to whether I'm there or not? Why the wink emoji? Has Garry told him how I feel about him? Has Tom told Garry how he feels about me? Is this a date??* I've never known an emoji to bring such emotional turmoil! My head spun. I was used to my head spinning, but this was different. This wasn't a thunderstorm with gale force winds and torrential rain. This was more like, lightning. (Insert screaming emoji).

All week, I was a total nervous wreck. I bit all my nails down to the quick and the stress made me break out in spots, typical! Every time I thought about seeing Tom again, I got so nervous, I could hardly breathe! As always, I went over every possible scenario in my head, playing out word for word, everything he could possibly want to say to me after all this time.

Scenario 1 – He loves me. I walk into the bar alone, turning heads and silenced voices as I walk, *no float,* through the crowds like a movie star. I see Tom in the distance, laughing and telling jokes with Garry and Scotty at the bar, crowds of people around him, drinking in his charisma, like moths to a flame. He graciously smokes a cigar, perfectly complimenting the single malt he swirls in his other hand. Suddenly, he sees me through the corner of his eye; his laughter stops, he grows silent. He stares at me in disbelief through the crowd, which is parting like the red sea, permitting a stretch of clear air between us.

He slowly rises from his bar stool, dispassionately waving off anyone else who hovers to him, seeking his attention. His eyes never leave mine. He glides through the crowds of people, each of them pausing as he passes, eager to see the scene play out as he moves with purpose towards me. He moves to within inches from me. I can feel his breath brush my lips as we stand face to face, eyes locked, as if nothing or no one else in the world existed. Another half-step. I feel his body press solidly against mine. My heart races, my chest heaving for breath.

"What took you so long?"

He rushed his lips hard against mine, pulling the rest of my body firmly against his. I let myself collapse into his arms, allowing him to hold my weight, stopping me from falling. Safe, that this is how things were always meant to be. Knowing that I would always be safe.

The problem with scenario 1: Our lives, as much as my overly vivid imagination would like them to be, are *not* scenes from *Casablanca*.

Scenario 2 – He loves me not. I walk into the bar after hours, *days* in fact, of pruning and polishing, and nobody blinks an eye. I see Tom in the distance, happy and laughing with his friends. He doesn't notice me, so I quietly join the crowd around him. When he finally meets my eye, he nods his head, solemnly greeting me as a past acquaintance, before turning back to his joke, completely unmoved.

"So, as I was saying," he continues.

My world crumbles to his unknowing and uncaring feet.

The likelihood of Scenario 2: Considering that the last time we met was not a million miles away from this scenario, and the fact that he was probably either forced, or tricked into this meeting; this is probably the most likely outcome.

Scenario 3 – He hates me. I walk into the bar and his attention turns immediately to me. Hate fills his eyes. He moves forcefully through the crowd, pushing people out of his way, desperate to reach me. I wait with open arms, ready to throw them around him. When he reaches me, he screams malice into my face. He spits that he never wants to see me again, that he wishes he had never met me.

Scenario 3: hurts.

I tried to suggest to Garry that this wasn't such a good idea, that Tom probably hates me.

"He almost definitely doesn't hate you," he answered.

'Almost definitely?' did not ease my concerns. But I had let Tom go so many times already, I had to try one last time. And now that so much else was different, maybe we would be destined for Casablanca after all.

Eventually, after waiting for what felt like a month, Tom and I's 'date' finally came. I met Garry, Scotty and Tom on the bus, and we headed into town to see *Lord of the Rings: Two Towers*. It was easily the most awkward evening of my life, with neither me nor Tom being willing or brave enough to make the first move and actually talk to each other. After the movie, we went to Tom's house, where we all got stuck into a long-awaited bottle of tequila. Garry and Scotty did their best all night to relieve the unbearable tension between Tom and I, but what we all really needed, was tequila. I knew that he spent all night wanting to talk to me, just as I did. All night, every time his eyes met mine, they darted away like a rabbit caught in headlights. He reminded me of the first time we met. After an hour or so of tequila shots, he started to shift, inch by inch, closer to me.

"Can I talk to you for a second?" He couldn't look at me.

"Of course." I couldn't look away.

He led me silently out of his bedroom, where we left Scott and Garry, and into the bathroom next door for privacy. We entered the dark room and as I raised my hand to turn on the light, he grabbed it.

"Don't. It's easier in the dark."

I lowered my hand, still held by his. Until suddenly, as if he realised he was holding my hand, he released me, like the touch of my skin burnt him. I looked up at him. Now, he was looking straight at me.

"I, I missed you." Tension hung so thick in the air, I could hardly breathe.

"I missed you too."

"I wanted to call, but I didn't know what to say. I didn't think you'd want to know. I'm so sorry. I should never have let you leave without telling you."

His voice choked and struggled, like he was desperate for air. He stopped; I could almost see the words stick in his throat. His breathing was heavy, he squirmed with panic. My own heart pounded hard and fast in my chest, my mind raced with possibilities, I heard myself screaming at him in my head *'Oh my god just say it!'*.

Tom took a deep breath and steadied himself; he looked me dead in the eye.

"I love you. I've always loved you."

He looked like he was going to collapse. I felt like I might too. My whole body flipped in one motion, my heart moved rhythmically between my mouth and my stomach. For a few moments, all I could do was stare back at him, speechless. Then I realised, some actions speak louder than words.

I leaned into him, pulling his face down towards mine. I pressed his lips to mine so quickly that neither of us had time to change our minds or bottle out. The world stopped turning, standing still in the moment alongside us. I always imagined Tom and I's first kiss to be soft, and gentle, and loving, and it was. But I never imagined that it would be so full of passion. After spending so long wanting each other, denying ourselves this pleasure, now, we were hungry for one another. I've never experienced a kiss like this. It was soft but hard, loving and soft but passionate and hungry. When our lips finally parted, we were out of breath. I felt dizzy, overwhelmed with every emotion I've never felt before in my life.

People always say that when you lose one of your senses, all of the others become heightened. Like when a blind man can hear conversations from the other side of a crowded room. Like when you close your eyes on a sunny day and suddenly the birds in the trees sing louder, filling in the sky with song. Or when a kiss in the dark sets all of your senses on fire at once.

"I love you too."

We stood together for what seemed like forever. His hands were around my back and my waist, my shoulders, my neck, my cheek. His hands danced over my skin, leaving trails of electricity everywhere they touched. He explored my whole body like a foreign land that he'd only ever seen in pictures. I was happy to let him. His eyes followed his hands as if he couldn't quite believe this was happening. I ran my fingers through his long hair, thinking of how many times I'd wished I could, but couldn't. His hair was like silk, just as I always imagined it would be. And now, standing here alone, together, in the dark, everything fell into place and we became one, just as we were always meant to be.

I don't know how long we stood in each other's arms in the dark. I lost count of the amount of times we gave in once again to our hunger and kissed, again and again. I always worried that if this ever happened that it would be awkward, two friends crossing boundaries. But it wasn't awkward at all, it felt like this was how things were always meant to be.

Every minute that we had spent together over the past two years rushed through my mind. I thought of the first time our eyes met over a shared chemistry textbook, of the sparks that flew between two people who had never even spoken. I thought of the day in the graveyard when his grip stopped me from slipping away completely. I remembered all the times that he sung me to sleep over the phone, when I wished so much that he could hold me while he did so. And now here he was, holding me, like he never wanted to let me go, like I was the only thing he had ever wanted.

After we had kissed enough to make up for all the times we couldn't, we sat in the dark and talked. We talked for hours. We talked of how life could be, how it *should* be, now that we were finally together. We talked of how we would leave, together, and never look back. We talked about how, years in the future, we would still sit alone, together, just as we did in that moment. We talked about how we would never need anything or anyone else, not luck nor money, because we had each other, and nothing else mattered. By the time we emerged from the darkness of the bathroom, it was daylight. Eventually, it was time to go home, and Tom walked me hand in hand to the bus stop. Leaving him then felt like the hardest thing I had ever done in my life, and I knew I would count every minute until I could be in his arms once again.

The following night, I went back to Tom's for our 'second date'. I was so nervous seeing him again. I had no idea if he was going pounce on me and carry on where we left off as soon as he opened the door, or if we would just carry on as we had always been. I hadn't heard from him since I left his house the night before. I had no idea how he was feeling.

We decided to go for the latter and spent the night acting as if nothing had happened at all. He seemed even more nervous and shy than usual, but I was no less nervous than he was. If my head was a mess, then it was fair to say that his probably was too. Overnight, we had gone from estranged best friends to destined lovers, and neither of us knew how to handle it. I spent the evening desperate to throw my arms around him and kiss him, again and again, just as we had the night before. But even after Tom's shock confession of his undying love, I couldn't shake the fear that had consumed me since the day I knew I loved him, that he didn't feel the same way, that opening that box would ruin everything. So instead of spending the evening together in the throes of passion, we spent the night just like we always had; talking nonsense, listening to music and avoiding any form of physical contact. At the end of the night, as he walked me to the bus stop to wait for my bus home, I knew that I had to be the one to say something, anything. If we didn't talk about it tonight, I knew there was a risk that the whole situation would pass us by and be left in the past, because even now, we were both still too afraid to say how we felt. I felt that familiar feeling as the air grew thick around us, as I worked up the courage to bring up what had happened between us.

"So, do you think we should talk about what happened the other night?" I tried to tread gently.

"Probably." Tom's eyes darted away from me.

He reminded me of a child who had just been caught stealing sweets from the local corner shop.

Silence.

"Well, I was just kind of wondering if you, you know, regret what happened?"

"No. Do you?"

"No."

The silence between us was deafening.

"So, you still feel the same way?"

"I have felt this way since the minute I met you. I'm not going to stop now."

Now he was looking at me. His nervousness vanished. He took both of my hands in his, and for a few moments, we simply enjoyed the touch of each other's skin.

"I want to give you everything. Everything we talked about. I want to commit *every* bit of me to making you happy. I just don't know how to do it. I feel like, I love you *so* much, but I just don't think that I can give you enough. I don't know how; I don't know if I can."

He gripped my hands tighter, desperate not to let me move away. He pulled me towards him so there were only inches between us. He moved his head down towards mine. But instead of kissing me, he moved his face around to my cheek, his lips hoovering over my skin, looking for a place to make contact. His lips moved so softly over my cheek, up to my temple and down to my neck, his hot breath sailing over me like a warm breeze. My body screamed for him to kiss me. His lips brushed over my skin like a feather. Knowing that he was so close, yet still not close enough, set me on fire. Just as I thought I couldn't take anymore, he pulled back from my neck to face me. He looked me deep in the eyes and I could *feel* him whisper "I love you". I didn't need to hear the words; I could *feel* them on his breath.

Our silence was broken by the sound of the bus pounding down the road towards us. Suddenly, the love in Tom's eyes dissipated and he looked distraught, like this was our final goodbye. I knew he was terrified of what was about to happen between us. By this point, I knew what he wanted, he made it quite clear. But sometimes just *wanting* something, isn't quite enough.

"I'm scared too," I reassured him. He shook his head, unassured.

"I want this. You have no idea how much. I just don't know how to. I don't want to hurt you. I just don't think I can do this."

"You could never hurt me. This is all I want. You are all I want. It's always been you."

We both smiled. Finally, the ice started to break. I reached my hand up and ran my fingers through his hair. Silk.

"We can just take things slow. See what happens. We've waited this long."

He nodded.

As the bus pulled up to the stop, we reluctantly prepared for separation. He held onto my hand tightly until the very last moment when I stepped up onto the bus.

"Call me – when *you're* ready. I'm not going anywhere, not this time." I tried again to reassure him as the bus door closed, cutting off the invisible link between us.

As the bus pulled away, I felt my heart break, like part of me knew, that it was over before it began.

But that couldn't be it. Tom and I have been in love with each other for two years. Everything up to this point has kept us apart. Surely fear and uncertainty wouldn't be the thing to finally make us quit? Even Romeo and Juliet made it in the end. Sort of.

But if he wanted time, I would give him time. If he wanted space, I would give him space. And when he was ready to want me, I would be there, ready and waiting, just like I always had been.

For the first few days, I hung religiously by the phone waiting for him to call, waiting for him to tell me that he'd been an idiot, that wild horses couldn't keep him away from me. I even took the phone with me to the bathroom, just in case I missed his call. Every minute I waited, I imagined the moment we reunited, only this time, it wasn't a scene from an old movie, it was a scene from my own life, it just hadn't happened yet. I pictured him running the three miles from his house to mine as if his life depended on it. Running, desperate to catch me in his arms and hold me like he would never let me go. For the first few days, the scene re-ran itself over and over in my mind as I waited. But the longer I waited, the fainter the picture became.

I relived our night together over and over. I closed my eyes and felt his lips softly move over my cheek, my neck, my shoulders, leaving a trial, tingling along my skin like threads of silk. I felt him hold me so close, that I could feel his heartbeat in sync with mine as he told me he loved me, that he would always love me. Then when I opened my eyes again, I heard him tell me that he was sorry, that he wasn't ready. At first, I was in ecstasy, knowing that he loved me, that one day he would be ready, and we would be together like I now knew we both wanted. But the more I replayed our conversation, the more I heard all the things which at the time, I never let myself hear.

"I just don't think that I can give you enough. I don't know how. I don't know if I can."

His words twisted and turned each time I heard them until they started to tear me apart.

"I just don't think I can do this."

I didn't hear it the first time. I didn't want to believe that this could all be happening so wrongly. It wasn't meant to be this way. But the longer I waited, the more time I had to question everything he had said. If he wanted to be with me, then why did we even have to have that conversation? Why is he not here now? The longer I waited, the more I began to wonder, was he was asking for time for him to be ready, or time to let us both forget what had happened between us? Had we broken up before we had even begun?

After about 2 weeks, I stopped waiting by the phone. I still jumped every time it rang, but I knew in my heart that it wasn't going to be him. He was never going to call. He didn't want time, he wanted out. This time, I knew he was gone for good, and I didn't even know why. I had finally let down my wall and given him everything, and with no defences left in place, there was nothing to stop the storm from engulfing me completely. All I could do was let it. Losing Tom knocked the last bit of breath out of my body, and now, I was happy just to let myself drown. I had spent years trying to survive in a world surrounded by inequality, ruthlessness, malice, hatred. And every day I kept breathing. Every day I forced myself to keep breathing because at least I knew I was not alone. There was always someone else out there, fighting to keep their own head above water, and that one day we would find each other, and we would both be saved. Even when I couldn't see him, I always knew he was still right there next to me. Even when he was gone, he was always reminding me that even when you're walking in total darkness, if you have someone to guide you through, one day you will find light at the end of the tunnel.

Last night, I dreamt of Tom and I, lost at sea. It was dark and the sea mist surrounding us made it seem like we were the only two people in the entire world, like the rest of the world had been swallowed up by the mist and we were the only ones left. We had no boat, no paddles; all we could do was cling to each other and keep kicking. Any time either of us ran out of fight and sank below the water, the other quickly pulled them up and into the air. Then suddenly, Tom stopped kicking. He let go of my hands and drifted away into the mist. I screamed for him. I searched frantically all around me, but he was gone. Swallowed by the dark world around me. For a while, I kept kicking, desperately trying to hold my head out of the water. But I wasn't strong enough without him, and eventually, I drowned.

Chapter 16 – It Never Rains, It Pours

After losing Tom all over again, all I wanted to do was run away. I wanted to get as far from away from everything as I possibly could. Just leave and never look back. I didn't even know myself anymore. I didn't even want to. What was the point? Turns out though, that leaving, requires having somewhere to go to. Every now and then, I would wait until everyone was asleep, then I would pack my backpack and I'd leave in the middle of the night, drenched in tears and panic. I walked around a bit. Sit on a park bench for a while, lost. And then I always ended up home and back in bed before anyone even knew I was gone. The only thing more depressing than hating yourself and your life so much that all you want to do is walk away from it and never look back, is being stuck there, because you have nowhere else to go to.

I grew so tired. I was tired of living in a world I hated. I was tired of being a person that even I didn't care lived or died. Every day I felt like I was fighting a war. I was fighting against a 10,000 strong army of soldiers, and now I was fighting alone. I struggled to remember, to find a reason why I was even bothering to try.

But I didn't want to be this way. I wanted, more than anything, for things to be different. I told myself that if I left, if I could start over somewhere new, where I could be *someone* new. By surrounding myself with people who had never met me, I could be anyone I wanted to be. I would magically transform myself, like a butterfly from a cocoon, into the fun, life-loving girl that I knew I could be, and nobody would ever need to know how pathetic I was in my old life. But I had tried that once before already. I didn't understand at the time that every time I ran, my problems always followed.

After losing Tom, I felt so alone. But in reality, I was never alone. There was always some guy willing to keep me from myself, even if it was for the wrong reasons, I didn't care. I was already so alone in my own mind, that the only thing that kept me moving each day was knowing that at least on the outside, I was needed, I was wanted. Surely it was better to have the appearance of being loved, than to not be loved at all.

Over the next year or so I dated, good guys and bad ones. I was no longer looking for love, only distraction from myself. I was falling down yet another spiral, only this time I had no one around me to blame but myself. When I was alone, I started to think. Voices started chattering in my head, whispering conspiracies against me. They told me that I was not wanted, that the people around me would be better off without me.

But love shouldn't be about needing someone to be there for you. Love should be about wanting, more than anything, to spend every waking moment of your life making someone else happy. It should be about doing everything you possibly can to keep them safe, to make them feel loved, like they are the only person in the entire world. Love should be self-less. But for me, it was no longer self-less. I wanted *them* to care about me; I needed *them* to want me. I wanted them around so that *I* felt loved, so that I never had to be alone. And I was never alone, I never needed to be. There was always someone just as selfish as I was, waiting to jump into the empty space next to me to satisfy their own reasons. I wasn't stupid, I knew what I was doing. I was being used the same way that I was using them. But it was better that way. This way, no one got hurt. I thought that

Jamie and I would be together forever. Despite the stained memories of our gruesome demise, we loved each other once. Not for selfish reasons, but for real. And then when I met Tom, I fell even harder, harder than I ever thought possible. And when we finally made it, after so long of being kept apart, after overcoming so many obstacles, I thought that my true love was finally happening. Only I didn't get the happy ending that I had imagined so many times, I was starting to feel like maybe I didn't deserve it.

When I was a child, desperate to grow up and fall in love, I was a hopeless romantic. I watched movie after movie, where the hero and heroine always fell madly in love and lived happily ever after, no matter what obstacles stood in their way or what the cost would be. I had been 'in love' with somebody ever since I could remember, always waiting to find the one that would finally fall as head over heels in love with me as I was with them, or at least the idea of them. In primary school, the love of my life was a boy called Scott Govan. He was the most beautiful boy I had ever seen in my life. He had long chocolate brown hair that hung down in front of his face, just about covering his dark brown eyes. Every time he flicked his hair back out of his face, my heart would melt. His permanently tanned skin looked like it would taste of smooth milk chocolate. But 2 years my senior, he didn't know I existed. We were friends, but I knew that no matter how much I followed him around, and no matter how sweetly I fluttered my eyelashes at him, he would never love me. Every day, it would break my heart to have to be with him, but not get to be with him. Then one day, I found out that he was moving to Texas, 5000 miles away. I was distraught. I sat in my bedroom and cried for days. I wouldn't eat, I wouldn't go to school, I just cried. I wrote letter after letter to Scott, desperate to tell him of my undying love for him. Each one I threw away into a crumpled heap. No words were ever good enough to describe how I felt about him, I never sent Scott any of those letters and I never got the chance to tell him how I felt. If love was really this painful, then I wanted nothing to do with it. At the age of 11, I had sworn off men and love, and resigned myself to dying unloved and alone.

When I was 12, Leonardo DiCaprio restored my faith in love once more with the release of Romeo and Juliet. I was mildly obsessed. Not only with Leo, as was every other girl in my year, but of the love story. I saw the film a hundred times or more, I read the play and memorised all of Juliet's part, on the chance that maybe one day, I would need it. My imagination grew wild at the idea of being swept off my feet by my Romeo, destined to be my forever love. I pictured scenes in my head of the first time we met. I would be at a party or walking round a supermarket, and there he would be. Hiding behind cereal displays, trying to sneak a look without being seen. As soon as I turn around, he would hide, pretending not to see me, pretending I hadn't seen him. He would continue to stalk me, all the time falling deeper in love with me every time I caught his eye before he shrunk away. Then eventually we would meet face to face, an aisle between us, a wall of cereal, a pallet of fruit, a fish tank. But nothing could keep us apart. When we reached the end of the aisle, stood face to face, no more barriers between us, he would steal my hand between his.

ROMEO:
    (Taking JULIET'S hand) If I profane with my unworthiest hand
    This holy shrine, the gentle sin is this:
    My lips, two blushing pilgrims, ready stand
    To smooth that rough touch with a tender kiss.

JULIET:

    Good pilgrim, you do wrong with your hand too much,

    Which mannerly devotion shows in this;

    For saints have hands that pilgrims' hands do touch,

    And palm to palm is holy palmers' kiss.

ROMEO:

    Have not saints lips, and holy palmers too?

JULIET:

    Ay, pilgrim, lips that they must use in prayer.

ROMEO:

    O then, dear saint, let lips do what hands do:

    They pray, "Grant thou, lest faith turn to despair."

JULIET:

    Saints do not move, though grant for prayers' sake.

ROMEO:

    Then move not, while my prayer's effect I take.

    Thus from my lips, by thine, my sin is purged.

He kisses her.

JULIET:

    Then have my lips the sin that they have took.

ROMEO:

    Sin form my lips? O trespass sweetly urged!

    Give me my sin again.

He kisses her again.

JULIET:

    You kiss by the book.

I grew up thinking that love was the beginning and end of everything. Yet the first time I truly found it with Jamie, it wasn't long before I let it all fall apart when I met Tom. Before I met Tom, Jamie and I were in love. We wanted to spend the rest of our lives together. And then I ruined it, by letting myself fall for someone else. As much I loved Tom in the end, I loved Jamie first. Did I let that happen? Could I have stopped it? My whole life, I had blamed myself for everything that had ever happened to me. It was my fault for being weak. It was my fault for letting the darkness consume me. It was my fault that I wasn't strong enough. Did I hate myself so much that I caused the destruction of my first true love, the one thing that I truly wanted, and had wanted since I was so young, because I felt I didn't deserve it?

I tried so hard to separate myself as much as possible from real life. An endless session of binge drinking, unruly all-night parties and a stream of meaningless 'relationships' that do nothing more than pass the time. Time till what? Resignation? Defeat? A welcomed rest in peace?

One benefit of my ever-changing relationship status was the frequent chance to reinvent myself, to try again. Sometimes I wondered if I longed more for the next chance to become someone else, than I did to feel loved. Each time I began a new relationship, I began it as a new person, each time thinking I had learnt from my past mistakes. I tried time and time again to get closer to the person I wished I could be, rather than the person I was. I hated the person I had become. I knew it wasn't really me, it was like I had become another person. *This* person was exhausting, all-consuming. I didn't want *this* person around anymore than anyone else did. The things I heard them say in my head, I agreed with them.

Every time I tried to re-invent myself, I tried to leave that person behind me. But it never worked. And each time I failed, I could feel the hands around my throat tighten more and more every day. I was waiting for the day that all the air is squeezed from me, leaving me cold and lifeless on the floor. I knew in every bone of my body that that day would come. It was simply a waiting game. But if I could live out my days in a haze of alcohol and passion, then I wouldn't have to feel each day that I was moving closer and closer to my own death.

Then one day, a funny thing happened. I realised that maybe the world wasn't against me, maybe *I* was against myself. I had spent most of that year drinking my time away, hating my life so much that I wished I was dead. I thought there was no good left in the world. I couldn't see the point anymore in waiting around for something that was never going to come. I was so sick of thinking I'd found something good, only to have it smashed to pieces. But maybe the first mistake I was making was waiting around for *it* to come to *me*. Maybe there *was* good all around me, maybe I just couldn't see it. I couldn't see it, because I wasn't willing to look. I was so set in my mind thinking that this is the way my life is, and this is how it will always be, that I wasn't willing to see it. But then, one day, I saw it.

One weekend, my head was in a particular mess, I spent the weekend trying my hardest to find some peace away from myself: by getting lost. Sunday morning, I woke up on the living room floor of a flat that I didn't recognise, surrounded by people that I didn't know, and covered in blood. I had no recollection of how my wrist got cut, at first, I assumed it was self-inflicted. I later remembered an accident involving an over-enthusiastic school friend I hadn't seen in a while, and an unfortunate ceramic plant pot which also didn't fare so well. When I woke up, dazed and confused, I had no idea where I was. And when I walked out into the street in last nights' clothes and makeup, it took me a while to figure out which direction to start walking. Eventually, I started walking back towards the bus stop home. My head was spinning. A combination of shame, self-hatred and alcohol. *This is probably what rock-bottom feels like.* All of a sudden, it started to rain. The kind of heavy rain that catches you off guard and makes everyone around you shriek and run for cover. But when you've got nothing left to lose, what difference does a little rain make? I stood in the street, fast flooding with water, and let the rain drench me. I let the water soak through my clothes until it smothered my skin. I felt tiny pinpricks of cold water hit my bare skin, striking at my flesh as it tried to penetrate my skin and flood my body. I pictured what would happen when the water flooded my body. My thick, red blood would grow thin, watered down until it washed away completely and only the rainwater remained to pump through my empty veins. My organs filled with water, slowly swelling like a water balloon with the rising water invading every crevice. And just like a balloon, when you overfill it, it will eventually collapse under the pressure.

But as soon as I felt the water striking me, I felt it drip back off me to the ground. On the outside, I was soaked. The water heavied my clothes and flooded my skin. But on the inside, I was still dry. On the inside, I was still the same. Water didn't pump through my veins, filling my organs, blood did. I wasn't going to collapse under the pressure, my body was holding me up, *I* was holding me up. And no matter how much it rained, it never got in. My skin stopped the water penetrating like it was protecting everything that hid beneath it. I held my hands out in front of me, ready to catch the rain that fell into my palms. I watched as the water hit again and again, with every force it had, and then rolled down my wrists, defeated. My waterproof skin didn't stop the water from striking. It didn't lessen the pain of the pin-prick sensations the rain created all over my skin, but it still stopped the water from affecting me on the inside. It was a nice feeling to think that my skin would protect me from the elements in this way. But at the same time, it made me sad, wishing that somehow I could protect the rest of me. And that even if I could somehow find a way to shield my mind from myself and my own destructive thinking, I couldn't change the fact that it's not only me that needs to change. I can't help but think, in a world that is so cold and uncaring and heartless, why try?

And then suddenly, as if I had somehow signalled to the world that it had gone too far, it took a step back. I was in my own world, staring into my palms as the rainwater ran over them, when suddenly the water stopped. I looked up from my palms, which were no longer catching the water that fell on me, and into the smiling face of an old man.

"Here," he said as he thrust the stick of the umbrella into my hands. "You look like you could use this."

He smiled. The kind of smile that reached up from the corners of his mouth and into his eyes. And before I could move my mouth to thank him, he vanished back into the rain, leaving me standing alone on the pavement once more. Only this time, I was sheltered; protected.

I'm not particularly religious, not at all, in fact. But if I were, it would be the answer I had been looking for; it would have been a sign from God.

Or maybe it was a reminder that however dark things may seem, there is still goodness in the world, but you have to be willing to see it. Maybe you have to get caught in the rain to remember how good it feels to come back in out of it. Maybe it was a reminder to keep going, because one day, the rain will stop and the sun will shine once more.

"Adversity is like a strong wind. It...tears away from us all but the things that cannot be torn, so that afterward we see ourselves as we really are, and not merely as we might like to be." —Arthur Golden, Memoirs of a Geisha.

Chapter 17 – A Whole New World V2.0

About a year after moving back home, I met my next big love. We fell in love almost instantly. After just one night together, I knew that this time things would be different, my faith in love was restored.

Mark worked in the local pub and was friends with some of my old school friends. I had heard about him often, but since I had spent the last year either hiding away or in a self-induced coma, I had never had the pleasure of meeting him.

After my encounter with the old man that saved me from drowning in the rain, I felt like I had finally woken up. I was trying hard to move forward. I knew now that it was me, holding myself back. I let everything in and let it fester. I was starting to understand that it is my own responsibility to change my life. It is my responsibility to make myself happy. So that's what I was going to do. I was no longer drowning myself in tequila or hiding away from the world in a cloud of smoke, I was trying my hardest to be part of it, to find reasons to *want* to be part of it. I can't say that it was easy, but it was certainly better than fighting my way through darkness and self-pity every day. I was determined I could leave my past behind me and move on. I was actively spending each day trying to find happiness, contentment, on my own. I was even practicing in new mantra, – *"if there's a will, there's a way"*. If I can *will* myself to be happy, then one day it will come.

Since moving home, I had rekindled some of my old friendships, some *safer* ones. The friends I left behind at the flat, they weren't safe. I know now that none of them ever meant any harm and it certainly wasn't anyone's fault but my own that I ended up having to crawl back out from that rabbit hole, but they also didn't care enough to stop me. I missed them every day, but I knew I was better off without them. Now with my new circle of friends, there was no drugs, no 48-hour ragers, and no danger of losing myself so far that I couldn't find my way back. We still drank down the pub on a Saturday night, but now my social activities were expanding. We met for lunch and went to the cinema, even occasionally to the gym. It was refreshing to spend time trying to be part of something, rather than trying to get away from it. I was still on the outside, of course. But I'd rather be on the outside of a circle that looks out for one another, than on the inside of one that doesn't.

My main new partner in crime was Steven. We had been good friends before we left school, but when I moved into the city, he didn't follow like the others did, so we lost touch. But now we were making up for lost time and I couldn't ask for more. He reached out just when I needed someone the most and hadn't let go since. He integrated me into his own group of friends, our group of friends, and it was through him that I met the infamous Mark.

Steven was originally from the Wirral and moved up to Scotland with his family when he was a kid. He still had some friends down there, and even a girlfriend, so he went down to visit as often as he could. Steven and our other friend Kevin had decided one night in the pub that this would be a perfect excuse for a road trip, and after being invited along to join them, I couldn't have agreed more! It would be my first 'proper' weekend away and I felt like a kid on Christmas Eve, waiting for Santa to come. Steven, Kevin and I spent the entire night talking about how amazing our road trip was going to be! It was only after we had spent an hour trying to invent some new road trip games that we could play in the car that it eventually occurred to me, none of us could drive.

"How will we even get there? None of us can drive!"

"No worries, Mark's gonna drive. He has a car."

"Mark who?"

"You know Mark! Mark from the Mains!"

"I don't even know him!" Suddenly, I was nervous. Going on a road trip with a total stranger no longer sounded like quite as much fun.

"Don't worry, you will!" Steven and Kevin giggled together like they were sharing an inside joke. Now I was even more nervous!

A few nights later, Steven arranged for the two of us to go round to Mark's flat to introduce us and so we could get to know one another before having to spend the entire weekend together. I was so nervous on the walk round to his house, although I had no idea why. Mark wasn't a complete stranger; I had heard so much about him, I felt like I already knew him. And if he was popular with Steven and Kevin, then surely, he couldn't be that bad. But for some reason, I was still nervous. As soon as he opened the door, I understood why.

All my daydreaming of love at first sight, and here it was, everything I had been searching for, standing right in front of me. The light bounced off his short, spiked hair making him look like he wore a halo of light. His smile reached right into the depths of his eyes and I felt it light up the whole room. When his green eyes crinkled into his smile, looked straight into mine, I felt my stomach flip, and instantly, I knew I was in love. He held his gaze on mine and felt us connecting without any words being spoken. After a few seconds, Steven interrupted and brought us both back to earth, and Mark invited us into his flat.

I was surprised to see that Mark's flat was nothing like the flat at Union Grove, or like any other 20-something year-old's flat I had ever been in. It was clean, tidy, it smelled of a mixture of air freshers and Lynx. There were no beer cans lying on the floor, no cigarette burns on the carpet. Mark was no interior designer, but it was a real grown-up flat.

The rest of the night proceeded much like any other night in. We ate too much pizza, drank too much beer, and listened to music that was too loud. All night we laughed and joked and sang way to loudly to a rendition of *Queen* songs. I couldn't remember the last time I laughed so much and felt so much like myself, so at ease. But as much fun as I was having, all I wanted was for Steven to go home, so that I could get to know Mark. We spent the evening exchanging stolen looks, and I knew he was feeling the same way. Steven was getting drunker and drunker and had a reputation for passing out at parties. It was getting late in the evening and just as I was starting to think that it was probably only a matter of time, I looked over to find Mark staring straight at me. When I looked at him, he didn't look away. The way he looked at me made me feel wanted, and I could feel heat rising, I felt the butterflies flutter once again. Then his eyes started to crease as his smile turned into a devilish grin. He was up to something.

"I know," he said, his eyes never leaving mine. "Let's play...I never!"

He was still staring straight at me, but I knew exactly what he was up to. He made me feel shy and excited, as his eyes and his smile told me everything I needed to know. Steven, who was currently dancing away to himself, spun around in excitement, spilling half the contents of his beer can as he did.

"Yes!" he yelled, with the enthusiasm of a child in a toy store.

"OK, I'll go first," Mark said, his eyes still held on mine. Then he turned to Steven.

"First, a practice question. Never have I ever...said, after a night out, that I'm never drinking again."

We all drank.

"OK my turn, my turn!" shouted Steven enthusiastically. "Never have I ever, sent a dirty text to the wrong person!"

Both boys drank as I doubled over in laughter. Steven started to stumble, and Mark and I could see that Steven was reaching his limit. Mark caught my eyes again and shrugged, *Now you know something about me, your turn,* he said, still communicating with only his eyes.

"OK, my turn," I stalled for a moment, trying to think of a response to Mark's request that wouldn't be too embarrassing. "Never have I ever, pulled someone in a bar."

We all drank.

Is that it? Mark questioned me silently. I shrugged, not ready to give anything up.

"OK, let's crank this up a notch, shall we?" Mark moved to kitchen and returned with 3 shot glasses and a bottle of vodka. He set the glasses down on the table next to us and filled them to the brim with vodka.

"Never have I ever, thrown up on someone during sex."

I was shocked at Mark's question. But when I saw Steven's reaction, I realised that his question was targeted at Steven. Steven had obviously shared that unfortunate encounter with him before. Steven was an over-sharer, and I had heard plenty of stories myself!

"Oh man, that's not fair!" Steven picked up the shot glass and knocked it back, slamming the glass down onto the table. Two glasses remained. I looked at Mark, *I know what game you're playing. Then join me, why don't you?*

"OK, never have I ever, told someone that I was related to Arnold Schwarzenegger to get laid."

Another question specifically aimed at Steven. Mark winked at me and I felt my heart melt a little, knowing that I had done something that pleased him. *Atta girl!*

"Get to the chopper!" Steven yelled his best Arnie impersonation, holding the second shot glass above his head like a trophy.

He threw back the contents of the glass, slamming down the empty glass once again. He hurled himself onto the couch, His legs starting to struggle.

"My turn," announced Mark.

"No no no, wait a minute, wait a minute, it's my turn!" Steven slurred.

"Na man, you just went."

"Oh, OK then," Steven accepted, slumping back into the couch.

"Never have I ever, fallen asleep in a pub toilet and gotten locked in overnight."

"Aw man, you guys are picking on me!" Steven moaned. He drank down the third shot glass and slouched back into the couch again. Mark topped up the three glasses.

"No! No more," Steven waved his arm towards the vodka, his eyes half closed. "I just need a little break, 5 minutes! Then we go again...." Steven barely finished his sentence before his arm dropped to his side, his eyes closed, and his head fell back against the couch cushion. He had passed out.

"Every time." Mark chuckled. "Doesn't take much."

"Never has!"

We both laughed at how predictable our friend was and how infamously terrible he was at drinking.

But when the laughter stopped and I realised that this was it, we were finally alone, just like how I had wanted all night, I was suddenly nervous again.

"You wanna go for a walk?"

"Sure."

We left Steven asleep on the couch and went out into the night. It was one of those perfect nights, were there was a chill in the air that made your mind feel clearer. The stars shone bright above us, helping to light up the dark streets. We walked around for hours. I had worried earlier in the night that once we finally had time alone together, that we wouldn't find anything to talk about. But I had no reason to be worried. We talked for hours as we walked. We talked about everything and after just a few hours, I felt like I knew everything about him, and there was nothing I didn't like. He told me about his family and his childhood, how he was at school and now work, how he felt about life, about himself. He had insecurities about himself just like I did. It was the first time I had ever met anyone who talked so openly about all things that darkened his thoughts. It made it easier for me to open up too, and I found myself sharing things that I had barely even admitted to myself before.

We walked the streets that I grew up on, that I had seen every day of my life. But it didn't seem different that he was there with me. The more we talked, the more it felt like he had always been there. These were the streets that I had once been too afraid to walk down, but now I had no fear. As long as Mark was here with me, nothing or nobody could hurt me. I felt like he was guiding me through.

I took him through a walking tour of the village, showing him the places where I had learnt to ride my bike and where I had once taken a corner too fast and fallen off, skinning my knee. I took him to the playpark were Stuart and I used to meet each night, and the tree-swing in the woods where I spent most of my fourteen-year-old life. I took him to the garage I hid behind when I had my first kiss when I was ten, and the spot behind the graveyard that Tom had shown me, where you could see the whole town from the shadows. We walked around the grounds of my school and I explained the different territories and the groups that occupied them. I took him to the shop where I was attacked, and where I first lost my faith in humanity. In just a few hours, he knew my entire life. By about 3 a.m., we were starting to grow weary and rested a while on some steps outside the school. That was the moment I knew that my first instinct of Mark had been right. That first instinct that told me that I was in love.

For the first time that night, we had both grow quiet. A mixture of growing tired from a long night and knowing one anther enough to be comfortable in silence. We sat side by side, both conscious that our hips and thighs were touching, the first physical contact we had. My heart beat hard in my chest as I watched his hand creep closer to mine, holding back nervously. I moved my hand closer to his, an invitation. Then without any hesitation, he reached for my hand and held it softly between his. Bolts of electricity shot through me as if I was coming alive for the first time. He sat there with my hand in his, he didn't make any more moves. He was content simply holding my hand. We sat hand in hand, gazing at the stars, enjoying the calm and quiet of the night around us.

"Have you ever heard the story of Vega and Altair?"

"No."

The sound of his voice surprised me after so long sitting silently. As if I had fallen into a dream while I was awake, I had almost forgotten where we were.

"Vega was a princess, a goddess living amongst the stars. One day she flew down to earth and met a mortal boy and they fell in love. Vega promised to bring Altair up to the stars, so that they can be together. But when Vega's father found out, he was furious that his daughter could fall for a mere mortal when she was a goddess, and he forbid them from seeing each other. Then Vega's father brings Altair up to heaven, but places a river between them, keeping them apart for eternity. But every year, for one night a year, all of the magpies in the world fly up to heaven and their wings form a bridge over the river, allowing the two lovers to reach each other for one night a year only. It reminds me of Romeo & Juliet. They loved each other so much that nothing could keep them apart."

I was taken aback by his reference to Romeo & Juliet, the love story that I had let dictate the expectations of my entire love life.

"I didn't know you were a budding astrologer?"

"I'm not. I'm just a sucker for a love story."

It wasn't the traditional balcony serenade that I was expecting, but I knew right then that this was it. This was the true love that I had been waiting for.

He was no longer looking at the stars, and neither was I. He smiled so warmly at me; his eyes twinkled in the moonlight. *This is our love story,* his eyes whispered to me. He leaned slowly into me and my heart beat hard and fast. I could feel my heartbeat in my lips as they waited anxiously for his. When his lips finally met mine, I felt myself slip into euphoria as I let the moment take me over. His lips brushed against mine, so soft and gentle at first, like dipping a toe into water. His lips pushed harder as he dived in completely and I happily gave in to him. He moved his hands across my cheek and through my hair, his touch sent shivers down my spine and my whole body trembled, begging for his touch. When he pulled back, I was breathless, yet at the same time, I felt like he had breathed life into me. Mark laughed to himself.

"What's so funny?"

"I just had no idea that tonight would turn out like this. I feel like I'm going to remember this night for the rest of my life."

By the time the sun was bright in the sky and he was walking me to my house, hand in hand, I knew that overnight, my life had been changed forever.

*

A few weeks later, it was time for our weekend to Liverpool. By now, Mark and I had become inseparable, spending every night together and were looking forward to our romantic getaway – me, Mark and Steven. Since planning our trip, Steven had done nothing but talk about how much he couldn't wait to see his girlfriend, so we were looking forward to spending most of the weekend just the two of us. The weekend didn't quite go as planned.

The drive down there took about six hours and we had a blast with road trip games and Car-eoke. Steven and I were both eternally grateful to Mark, who did all the driving without complaining. When we got to the B & B, we were gutted to learn that when Steven had booked the trip, he booked a family room that the three of us would share, greatly limiting the amount of romance we would be getting on our 'romantic' getaway. Once we had checked in, we then spent the next hour or so 'helping' Steven decide what to wear, as he changed his shirt about ten times in an effort to find the 'perfect' look for when he was reunited with his girlfriend, Katy. Eventually, and after what felt like several hours, we were finally ready to hit the town!

Steven had found out in advance from Katy's friends where she would be, so that Steven could turn up and surprise her. By the time we arrived at *The Swan Inn*, Steven was beside himself with excitement. He was talking so fast, and since he had mysteriously developed a Liverpudlian accent since arriving in Liverpool, we were struggling to keep up with what he was saying. When we got to the bar, we were all buzzing. It was packed so full of people that we struggled to get through the door. But the friendly atmosphere and the good music made us confident we were all in for a good night. After about twenty minutes of searching the crowd, Steven finally spotted Katy and bounded towards her, beaming from ear to ear. He was so happy to see her that he failed to notice that she was sitting on another guy's lap. She quickly moved away from her mystery guy when she saw Steven, but it was too late, we had already seen her. Steven was so madly in love with her that he didn't even see the other guy's arm hugging her waist or him whispering sweet nothings in her ear, but Mark and I saw it.

For the rest of the evening, we watched as Katy squirmed away every time Steven pulled in close. We watched the other guy grow more and more pissed off as he kept his distance and eventually left in a huff. And at the end of the night when Steven had hoped to go home with Katy, she made an excuse that her grandmother was staying, and Steven ended up back in our family room with us. The next day, she had plans and couldn't see him. "That's OK", he reassured himself afterwards. "It's my own fault for just turning up without warning. I can't expect her to drop what she's doing for me. We'll still have a good time, the three of us, and I can come back and see Katy when she isn't so busy". Neither Mark nor I had the heart to tell Steven what we had seen at the club, or what was quite obviously staring him in the face, but that he refused to acknowledge. So instead, we spent the weekend trying our best to keep Steven's mind off the girlfriend that had obviously moved on but had forgotten to tell him. We saw the Beatles museum and the Victoria Dock and drank quite a lot of shots.

Mark and I spent the whole weekend waiting for the penny to drop. By the time we were on our way back home, it finally did. Just in time for our six-hour car journey to give Steven plenty of uninterrupted time to rant, rave, cry, mope and then finally, swear off women altogether. He called her from a service station en-route to break it off. When she didn't answer his call, he broke up with her voicemail. Six hours later and Steven had shifted through all the emotional turmoil that comes hand in hand with break ups, and by the time we dropped him off home, he was ready to move on, continuing his relentless, and somewhat unsuccessful search for true love. It was the swiftest, most efficient breakup I had ever seen. Like ripping off a plaster.

*

Over the next few weeks, Mark and I's relationship went from strength to strength, and before long, we had fallen hopelessly in love. I felt like I was living in a wonderful dream. And instead of the self-induced world-away I was used to, this time, I was high on life and love. Mark was everything I had ever wanted and more. I couldn't get enough. When I wasn't with him, I missed him so much it hurt. I wanted to be with him every minute of every day, and him me. I resented going to work every day because it pulled me away from him. I was the happiest I had ever been in my life and for a while, I had no fears, no darkness, it was just him, and me, and nothing else mattered.

Every time I thought about how perfect my life was, I couldn't help but laugh.

"What are you laughing at?"

"I'm just really happy."

"Why is that funny?"

"It just is."

I'd spent so many years thinking that I was destined to be miserable all my life. It was like I'd been living underneath a thick, black rain cloud, constantly following me around, raining cold, miserable rain on me 24 hours a day. And now, piece by piece, that cloud had been blown away and finally, the sun was shining through. I felt warm for the first time. And I felt safe. He made me feel safe. I told him everything about me, about how things had been in the past. And I had no doubt that if I was ever to fall again, he would be there waiting to catch me. I felt like this time I really was a new person, in a whole new world.

Just when I thought that I couldn't be happier, Mark proved me wrong, when he asked me to vow to spend the rest of my life with him. We were lying in bed one Sunday morning, like we did every Sunday morning, having the same conversion we had at the end of every weekend when I had run out of clean clothes and had to go home to get more. Only this week, the conversation ended a little differently.

"I need to go home today."

"No, don't. I don't want you to go." He pulled me closer, squeezing me tight like he never wanted to let go.

"I have to, I have no clean clothes for work tomorrow."

"So wear dirty ones."

I laughed at the suggestion, knowing that it wouldn't be the first time I took that option after not wanting to go home. "I can't, I need to go home."

"I don't want you to go home, ever. I want you stay here." He sat up to look at me, a look of seriousness came over his face. "I want you to stay here, live here. Move in with me?"

"Are you sure? I mean, we haven't been together that long, I don't want to rush you into anything." I was shocked at his question and wanted to make sure he was thinking it through. But inside I was screaming YES! YES! YES!

"I've never been more sure of anything in my life."

He took my hands between both of his, just like he did on the first night we met when I knew instantly that I loved him. Whenever he held my hands like that, a wave of calm would come over me as I remembered how safe he made me feel walking round the streets that night, streets that once terrified me.

"Then yes! I would love to live with you!" He had told me everything I needed to know, and I knew that this was right.

"Oh God, you make me so happy. I love you so much." He pulled me into him and hugged me hard against him. He held me so tight, like he was clinging on for dear life. "I just can't stand it when you're not here with me. I want to spend the rest of my life with you."

"I want to spend the rest of my life with you too".

I closed my eyes and melted into his embrace, enjoying the touch of his hand as he gently stroked my hair. Then suddenly, he pulled back to look at me again, his hands still holding tight onto my arms.

"I do, I want to spend the rest of my life with you."

He paused, his eyes looking over my entire body like he was trying to drink in every inch of me, committing me to his memory. Oh my God, what is happening here? I knew he was working up to something, but couldn't quite believe it. Inside, I continued to scream YES! YES! YES!

"Marry me." His breathing quickened and I could almost see his pulse race as he waited for an answer to the most important question he had ever asked. I needed no hesitation. I had my answer before he even asked the question.

"Yes! Yes!"

"Oh my God." He pulled me close once more, this time kissing me hard. "I'm gonna make you so fucking happy. I promise you. I will spend every single day of the rest of my life, making you as happy as you make me."

We stayed in bed for the rest of the day. The next day, I happily went to work in dirty clothes.

Chapter 18 – Driftwood

After getting engaged, Mark and I were living in domestic bliss. Having moved into Mark's flat, I began my latest challenge of becoming a domestic goddess; in training, to be the best wife I could be, and I was thriving. Mark had given me everything I ever dreamed of, and all I wanted to do was make him happy. I kept the house clean for him, I washed his dirty socks and I even learnt to cook a limited, yet excellent list of dishes. It was a very different lifestyle than what I was used to, but I was loving it, and I knew it was good for me. All I had ever really wanted was to be a normal, boring person, happily living a normal, boring life, and now I had everything I had ever asked for. I felt like I was now officially a grown up. Cohabiting with my fiancé, a decent job, real home cooked meals and a floor you could eat your dinner off.

Mark and I were happily practicing for the married life that lay before us. Now at weekends, instead of spending our time drinking down the local pub, we spent it at home, together. And it was the only place in the world I wanted to be. I loved our home. It was small and outdated, but it was ours. And after I moved in, Mark insisted that we redecorate, to make it a home for both of us. We spent our weekends painting and papering, out shopping for new bed sheets and throw cushions, which Mark never understood.

"Why do we need so many cushions? We don't even use them!"

"Because it's what people do."

I wanted so badly to make our home as normal and grown up as I could, a place to inspire *me* to be normal and grown up. And before I knew it, every wall was beige, every chair had a throw cushion and everything we owned had a place. Just like I did.

But it seemed that no matter how hard I tried, darkness always found a way to creep back into my life, my thoughts. It was all around me.

One day, I attended my first funeral. I didn't know the man who died, but Mark did. He was a regular at *The Mill,* the pub where Mark used to work, and he was a friend. I went to support Mark, to help him to show his respects, but I still felt twisted inside.

People filed one by one into the room, filling up rows upon rows of fold-away chairs. Waiting on each chair was a booklet. On the front of the book staring up at us, was a picture of Alan, bright with smiles, smothering a woman and two children in a bear hug. They were on a beach somewhere, a nice family holiday in the sun, not a care in the world. They looked like the type of family that would stay happy and in love forever. Their happiness beamed through the photograph like it could never be broken. People sat in silence, sombre, waiting to finalise the fact that the happy smiling family in the brochure, which was waiting for them on their seat, were broken, and would stay that way forever.

The room filled with people, young and old, not a smile between them. Then when the line of people finally stopped flowing in and everyone was sat waiting patiently, the women from the photograph walked up the aisle, a baby in one arm and gripping the hand of a toddler with her other hand. She wasn't bright and shining and in love like she was in the picture. Now she was shaken and lost and empty, as she made herway to sit in the front row, in front of her husband's coffin. I wondered if, during any of those blissful moments in the sun together, she ever imagined that one of those moments would be the last. Did she kiss his cheek and wish him a good day at work when he left the house for work that morning, like he did every day, but ended up in a coffin? Or did they argue? Did she nag him about leaving the toilet seat up or not putting his socks in the laundry basket? Are those socks still lying on their bedroom floor today?

She sat, staring at the coffin, completely unaware of anything or anyone else around her. The minister began to speak. He spoke of the tragic loss to have someone so young and loved taken from this world so suddenly. Her eyes never left the box where her husband lay, and she never registered a single word being said. The children, both still under five, sat bored and grumbling, blissfully unaware that they were at their own father's funeral. Every now and then, Alan's wife wrenched herself out of her catatonic state, into uncontrollable weeping and sobbing. Another woman did her best to calm her whilst an older woman tried to keep the children quiet and seated. As she wept, I saw every bit of hope she had ever had pour out of her like a river. I couldn't take my eyes off her. My stomach twisted in sympathy with every sound she made. As I watched her, I felt like I could feel everything she could feel, like I was absorbing her pain. The woman in the sunny photograph was gone. The happy family that spent that years' holiday on a beach somewhere, eating ice-creams and building sandcastles and giving each other bear hugs, was gone.

My mind started to race through images of all the happy snaps that Mark and I had saved up over the past year. I have them all neatly conserved in a photo album. Hundreds of bright smiles, ice-creams eaten and bear hugs, just like theirs. I felt familiar fingers wrap tight around my throat as the question crept into my mind. Would I one day have to sit in the front row, staring at Mark's coffin? Would I be just as oblivious to the room full of people sobbing over our happiest looking holiday snap?

For days, weeks after that, I couldn't stop thinking about the funeral. That family lost everything in the blink of an eye. Everything they thought they would have forever – love, security, friendship – that's all gone now. I bet that woman thought she was the luckiest woman in the world. Married to a wonderful man who would love and cherish her for the rest of her life. Beautiful children to raise into beautiful people alongside her loving husband, their doting father. Children that would love their parents unconditionally, forever. But now, instead of having all those things, she will spend her life grieving. Grieving for her husband, and everything they could no longer have. Her life as she had planned it was over. I couldn't shake the idea of what would happen if I lost Mark. I felt panic rising in my throat, constricting my breath just thinking about it. I was constantly thinking about it. And I was constantly struggling to breathe. I felt like my own mind was suffocating me. One day, Mark and I would get married, this should be the happiest time of my life, but my mind just wouldn't let it go. I was getting married to an amazing man who I loved, and I had no doubt that we would stay in love for the rest of our lives. I had everything I ever wanted; someone to stay by my side forever and never leave me. This should have been the happiest time of my life. Yet, all I could think about was losing it. My life was finally working out the way I wanted it to, and I was so scared that it was going to break. But I knew eventually it would, everything always does. Everything good in my life that had ever happened, eventually, just stops. This should be the happiest time of my life, but my own fears were ruining it.

I couldn't stand how reliant I had become on him being there. I started to hear that familiar voice in my ear, poisoning my thoughts with tiny seeds of doubt. Seeds that slowly grew and blossomed the longer we were together. *What if one day he did die, or what if we broke up? He doesn't really love me – I was wrong.* All I could think about was what it would be like to live without him. Doubts or not, I knew that if I lost him, my world would break in two, just like it's always wanted to. Everything I know would crumble around my feet, and I wouldn't be far behind. I couldn't live without him. But I also knew that it wasn't a good enough reason to keep on living with him. *Shouldn't it be easier than this? If I am so in love, why do I not feel happy?* It scared me how much I needed him. I wondered if it was normal to need someone so much that you can't even fathom the idea of having to live without them there to hold you up? This was so different from any relationship I'd ever been in. Maybe it was because we were getting married, maybe it was *meant* to be this way. But the total co-dependence and constant panic whenever he stopped for a pint on the way home from work without telling me, instead of coming straight home, was exhausting. I felt like my dependence of Mark had taken over so much of my mind, that I had morphed from a single person into part of a couple. I had an identity as part of that couple, but I felt like I was losing the one I had of my own.

As much as I couldn't stand the idea of being without him, I felt myself wanting to pull away. To protect the small part of me that was left outside from us. I always knew that eventually, everything would fall apart, and if I could distance myself from the blast site, maybe it wouldn't hurt so bad. Maybe I just didn't know how to exist without the darkness that had followed me my entire life. At least in the darkness I knew who I was.

Even from the beginning I was so scared all the time, that something was going to happen to rip it all apart. But part of me always knew that it would be me that did it. The last thing I wanted was to lose him. But the thought of that happening, constantly circling my head, poisoning my thoughts, was the very thing that was driving me away.

When Mark and I first got together, I thought this was it. All the clouds lifted, and the sun shone, just like I always knew it could. I thought it would shine forever, that the darker phase of my life was just that, a phase. I thought that now it was over, I could finally enjoy my life the way that I'm meant to, the way everyone around me seems to be able to do. But somehow, even my own happiness was turning against me.

I could feel the darkness trying to creep back in like a fog. I could almost see it in my mind, manifesting slowing on the horizon, drifting so gently, so silently that it was hard to tell whether it was real or just an illusion. Only this time, I was determined that things were going to be different. I wanted things to be different. I wanted to be able to enjoy all the good things that were finally happening in my life, and I knew that unless I tried to fight it, I would lose everything once again. I could feel my body fighting it. My legs kicking strong beneath the water, stronger than ever before, determined not to let me drown. I shut it out once before, and I could do it again. At least that's what I thought in the beginning. I had no idea how much more exhausting it would be fight back, rather than just let it consume me like it usually did. Even as I was telling myself I could do it, I could beat this, I was doubting that I even wanted to.

I had spent so many years hating myself, punishing myself for being weak, for letting myself feel pain when there was no pain there to feel. For letting that pain smother the happiest time of my life. What if it wasn't *me* that was wrong? What if *I'm* not the one who was broken? It was no longer that familiar little voice whispering in my ear, it was my own voice I was hearing. It was me that was asking. If it is this world that is broken, rather than me, how can it ever be fixed? How will it ever get any better. *It can't.*

Over the past few years, the world had changed so much that I was struggling to understand why I was fighting so hard to be a part of it. I grew up in a world where you could let your children run loose, not just in the street but around the entire village, because there was no question of their safety. Mothers did not warn their children *"Now kids, make sure you don't leave the garden, I wouldn't want you to be abducted and murdered by a paedophilic manic",* because there's most likely one living in the next street. Instead, you were reminded to wear a helmet whilst cycling, and stick to the green cross code. People left their front doors unlocked all day long because *this is a nice area and there's nobody going about*. In today's world, every day we hear of children being abducted from supermarkets, from their own bedrooms while they were sleeping at night. Their young faces plastered over the media for weeks or months to remind people that we do not live in a safe place. Reports of drug addicts breaking into the homes of pensioners, beating old ladies to death in their own homes, just to make some quick cash. Did she also think it was safe to leave her door unlocked because of the *nice* area she lived in? The world we live in today is one where it is not safe to walk down the street. One day, when I was walking to the bus station on my way home from work, I was blocked by police tape, diverting my route by several blocks due to a bomb scare in the city centre. People simply walking home after a long day at work, groups of girls out shopping with friends, friends and families out on the town celebrating a special occasion, tourists stopping to photograph the city architecture; in a moment, they could all be gone. Me, walking home from work, undiverted, I could be gone.

9/11 was the first time I had ever hear the word *terrorist* used as part of our everyday vocabulary. I was used to seeing terror attacks in movies and TV, and even in major events in history, but not during *my* life, not now. Now, it is a word that we hear every day, a word that strikes fear into the fearless and fills even the emptiest of hearts with sadness. Every day, it seems we hear this word in events and attacks and deaths all around the world. Every day we hear it. And every day we can see how changed the world has become. How *we* have changed, to protect ourselves from it.

I felt like every time I looked around me, I saw a little part of humanity being lost. It was all around me. And no matter how hard I, or anyone else tries to hide from it, it's there. It's always there. I see children dying by the hundreds, thousands, in wars that no one really understands why we're fighting. Yet, we continue to fight anyway. Young men, taught that fighting in war lands, killing innocent, as well as guilty people, will make you worthy, give you a reason to be proud. I see soldiers sent to these wars without reason, being taught that slaughter and brutality is the way the world needs to be to keep us safe. Yet, it doesn't seem to be working. Every day I hear of new tragedies. Suicide bombers shedding their mortality in the name of a god whom they claim condones the killing of innocent bystanders. Crazed gunmen opening fire in nightclubs, full of travellers enjoying their holidays. Children, being slaughtered in classrooms while they sit, eagerly learning their times tables. Buildings full of unknowing office workers being blown up while they write their morning to-do lists and wade through unread emails. I wonder what those workers were doing when it happened. Were they gossiping happily over a coffee break? Feeling guilty for having *'just one more'* chocolate biscuit? Had they worked tirelessly all morning to meet that deadline? Did anyone, just at that moment, walk out their boss's office, fist-pumping the air at the promotion they'd just been given? Did they collapse back into their desk chairs, sighing with relief, saying *"finally, all my hard work paid off."* And did any of those employees, those colleagues, wake up that morning and think, *"nah, think I'm gonna pull a sickie,"* and not turn up for work? How do *they* feel now? Knowing that some handsome twist of fate caused them to stay home that day, saving them from the towering inferno that incinerated every single person that they worked with every day. That every single person they worked with was gone, but somehow, they had been saved. And what about the mothers, who sent their children to school *that* day even though they pleaded *"but mummy my tummy hurts. I'm too sick to go to school today"*.

When I wake up every day, when I go to sleep every night, I couldn't stop myself from thinking about all of those who did not wake up that morning. I thought of their families, who wake up without them. I wondered if it's true that sometimes, when a grieving person first wakes in the morning, they forget. Those first few seconds, they forget that the person they love has been ripped unmercifully from them. They forget that the smile that once lit up rooms, the eyes that once sparkled mischievously when they were up to no good, the tell-tale twitch they have when they are bluffing at poker that only you know about, is gone now. For just a few sparing seconds each morning when they wake, do they forget that those things no longer exist?

I thought that all of this darkness was over, but I was wrong. Suddenly, I felt like it was only the beginning.

But if I had to fight, then that's what I would do. What other choice did I have? And in the meantime, I carried on as normal, like normal people do. Something I had already had a lot of practice at. And just like there always was, there was always a new distraction just around the corner.

*

Our flat was part of a small block of nine, just a ten-minute walk from the house I grew up in. Close enough to still feel at home, but far enough away to be making a life for myself. Our building was generally quiet. We didn't hear much of our neighbours, and most of them kept to themselves. Nobody was rude and everybody always greeted one another politely on the stairs, but never made the move to become anything more than people who occupy the same building, but in very different spaces. I always thought it was a shame. That it would have been nice to know our neighbours better.

Then one day we got a new neighbour, and everything changed. The very night that Ewan moved into the flat next door to us, he knocked on our door to introduce himself. It was the first social interaction that we had had with any of our neighbours, and it had been months since the last time we had had anyone round, so we happily invited him in for a drink. Just as he was walking through the doorway into our flat, he excused himself and ran back across the hall into his own flat. A few seconds later he reappeared, grinning from ear to ear and sporting an unopened crate of Tennent's.

"Wah hey hey!" he sang as he bundled past us with the beer, into our nice, quiet life. Mark and I exchanged looks and silent conversation, just as we had always been able to do, *Hold on tight, it's gonna be a long night!*

And so went our quiet, boring lives. Ewan came into our lives and our building like a whirlwind that nobody knew was coming. He knocked on door after door and within a few weeks, we knew the names of all of our other neighbours and much more at that. Ewan insisted on dragging us all to the local pub 'to get to know one another' one night, and we had never left. Nobody complained at the sudden appearance of social exchange between us all and I felt that, perhaps I was not the only one longing for something that I had left behind in a past life.

As much as I was enjoying practicing married life with Mark, part of me was finding it difficult to be this new person, in this new life that was so far apart from anything I had ever known before. I knew this was better for me. The drugs and drinking and parties had destroyed my mind as well as my body, and I knew that I could never go back to that. But part of me longed for it. Part of me still wanted to get lost.

I was excited to make some new friends. These were the first friends that I had met that didn't know me from any of my previous lives. They knew nothing about me, or my history and I felt free to be whoever I wanted with them. For the first time, I chose myself, or as much as I could remember of who I was.

Before long, drinks down the pub on a Friday each weekend escalated into 48-hour house parties on a more or less weekly basis. I felt my body struggle to keep up, but my mind wouldn't let it slow it. I knew what happened when everything stopped turning, so I just kept on spinning. It didn't take long for things to spiral out of control, just like they always did. Only this time, I knew better. I knew from the beginning that things would end up going too far, that I would end up losing myself, just like I had done so many times before. I wanted so badly to stop it from happening before it was too late, but in the end, I didn't. I let myself get carried away like a riptide. Even at the expense of everything I had spent the last year building, it was just easier that way.

I exhausted myself, to keep myself from having to return to my real life, which exhausted me even further. It's like the feeling you get when you're treading water. You kick and you kick, trying with all your might to stop your head from going underwater. You kick so hard that you feel like you should be able to propel yourself up and out of the water completely. But you never propel, you never get any higher. You try with all your will to move yourself forward, but no matter how hard you try, you remain in the same space. You kick and you kick and your legs ache with the effort of fighting against the tide, against this stagnant space that will forever keep you there. But if you stop kicking, if you rest your legs, if you stop fighting even for one moment, you sink, and you drown.

That's how I felt every day. Like I was constantly treading water. And every time someone tried to rescue me, I would let myself drift further away. I knew that Mark could see what was happening and he tried his best to coax me back onto dry land. He started suggesting that we don't go out at the weekend, that we just stay in together like we used to. I could see he wanted our old life back and I did too. I didn't want to lose Mark, and I knew that if I couldn't bring myself back to shore, I would drift so far away that I would never get back to him. So, after each weekend when the party was over and we prepared for a week of normal life, he suggested laying low the following weekend, and each weekend I would happily agree. But every week, by the time Friday came around, I just couldn't wait to get out of my own head and my own life, even if it meant hurting my relationship with Mark. I understand now that I was distancing myself on purpose, knowing full well what lay ahead at the bottom of the rabbit hole that had uninvitingly reappeared. This time, I was determined not to pull anyone down with me.

I didn't want to do the parties anymore. I didn't want to do anything anymore. But everything was so much easier this way. I didn't even want to go home anymore. I lived all week, waiting for the weekend when I could get out of my own life. And at the end of the night, I didn't want to go home. When I went home, I had to go back to real life. I had to go back to my life, with me in it, worrying myself sick that one day everything will break apart. When I was out with my friends, I could stop thinking, and just be me. More often than not, Mark would go home to bed and leave me partying at one of our neighbours. Sometimes, I preferred it. When it was just me, I didn't have to worry about what would happen when I no longer had Mark to hold me up. Maybe part of me was trying to kid myself into thinking that I didn't need him anyway. Here I was without him, and I was happy, or so I was leading myself to believe. After Mark left, there was nobody there to stop me. Nobody telling me to go home and nobody to stop me from drinking myself into oblivion. Some days, I even resented him. I resented that every Sunday I had to go home to the life, and the man, that was meant to make me happier than I'd ever been before, but in reality, all it did was remind me every day that I felt more incomplete than ever.

One night, in an effort to keep from going home and waking up in my own bed, I let myself fall asleep on Ewan's couch. When I woke up the next morning, I felt the presence of a warm body next to me, a head resting gently, sleeping on my shoulder, while mine rested against his. Still asleep, I felt around me and found his hand, resting gently next to mine. I ran my fingers over the soft skin of his palm and his fingers opened like a flower. Our fingers intertwined like it was the most natural thing in the world. Our hands squeezed together, trying to bridge the gap left between them. His fingers moved between mine, caressing each finger in turn, exploring every inch of my hand like a new foreign land. His touch left trails across my skin and I felt my body stir, waking to his. Suddenly, my mind caught up and I woke fully and jumped away from him, throwing his hand back. We both apologised profusely, caught in the moments between sleeping and dreaming, where it's too hard to tell what is real and what isn't. It was an honest mistake, that we had realised before it was too late. But I still went home to Mark, embarrassed and ashamed.

After that, it happened again and again. I had found a new distraction. I knew I should have stopped it before anything happened, but I didn't stop it, I encouraged it. Each weekend the parties would continue as normal and one by one, our neighbours would retire to their own beds, including Mark to the one we shared. I felt myself counting the hours until everyone else would leave, and Ewan and I could be close. During waking, we were friends and nothing more. But each night I slept on his couch we woke up closer and closer. He would be holding my hand, stroking my hair as I rested on his lap, or in full embrace, where I would wake to the touch of him gently stroking my back. We kidded ourselves that it was innocent, blaming our impaired judgement on last night's booze, or semi consciousness, that we were doing nothing wrong by simply holding hands and holding one another. Until one morning, we kissed. We were conscious, we knew what we were doing. I knew that now we were doing something wrong, but I let it happen anyway. I loved Mark more than anyone I had ever loved before, that hadn't changed. But for some reason, I couldn't stop myself longing for the closeness and attention that I got from Ewan each Sunday morning. I felt myself falling into the same trap once again. Only this time, I knew it was happening, and I knew that I was letting it. I was letting myself sabotage my relationship with the man I loved. I didn't understand why I did these things, but I knew by now that I did them. Maybe I was pushing away because I couldn't stand the thought of getting any deeper and then losing him. Maybe I still didn't feel like I deserved to be happy.

I thought that once I met Mark, everything had turned around. I thought that now I was where I was meant to be, that I would stop self-destructing. But nothing had changed. I was the happiest I had ever been in my life, and I still hadn't been able to stop myself falling into the same self-destructive patterns. I started to doubt that there was any hope left for me. If happiness couldn't save me, then what could?

After Ewan and I kissed, I knew I had to leave. I had leave them both before I destroyed them too. It would be the hardest thing I ever had to do, but I was caught in a cyclone of my own doing, and this time I was pulling others down with me. I had never been more sure of anything in my life, Mark and Ewan would be better off without me.

They would all be better off without me.

Chapter 19 – The Calm Before the Storm

The first thing I remember was white. When I woke up, everything was white. The air was so fresh, so clear. But this fresh, clear air was not my life. This was not my life. Fear raced through my veins and took over every muscle in my body, and I froze. Every hair on my skin stood on end amidst my panic. Maybe only for a second, any recollection of how I came to be in this strange, clear air had escaped me. Maybe only for a second, until it recaptured me and sucked me dry. Maybe only for a second, I wondered if maybe I was dead.

My skull pounded like a steel drum. Blurry images flashed with every throb of my head. A woman cried hysterically in the distance. Her voice echoed through me as if she was talking to me through a portal to another dimension.

"Oh God, what have you done? Why? Why did you do this?" a man shouted, his frantic voice stung holes like bullets through my head. *"Wake up! Please! Don't fall asleep!"* He burned through my thoughts like a demon burrowing into my mind.

It was all too much. The room began to spin, my body rejected the contents of my stomach and I vomited. I gasped to take a breath, but before I could, I vomited again, and again. The empty liquid forced its way out of my system and splashed onto the white linoleum floor below the white bed that I found myself in. My whole world was dazed. Whenever I tried to focus my vision, I vomited again. I wrenched uncontrollably, over and over before my body finally let up. As I stopped to breathe, I heard something below me crashing to the floor, a glass, knocked off the bedside table amidst the commotion of the liquid evil leaving my body. The noise got somebody's attention and a woman, also dressed in white, forced a bed pan under my chin to catch the rest of the bile that was inevitably to follow. I felt my body relax as it prepared for the next wave of sickness that I knew wasn't far away. It was just enough time for my mind to catch up with my body and realise where I was.

I was in hospital. For that moment, how or when I arrived there eluded me, but why, flooded my heart and drowned my soul. Before I could finish my first line of thought, my mere second of physical freedom was over and I was thrown back into a violent episode that took over my entire body. It turned my tired ache into a consistent sharp throb that gripped every bone in my body, every time I wretched. I quickly filled the bed pan, before another was thrust into its place. My body finally began to slow, and I quickly realised that the ache in my bones wasn't caused by the pain that came with the persistent vomiting, the ache came directly from my heart. An overwhelming stabbing that accompanied my realisation that I had hurt, beyond repair, the only people in the world who cared whether I lived or died, when I tried to take my own life.

As I regained control of my body, my mind took its place, racing with sounds and visions that I did not understand. The muffled sounds of the frantic woman's voice became clearer with each passing moment that I lay there. It was as if it was coming from a different world. Like some vivid dream where you remember some parts so perfectly clear but other parts, the parts that bring the story together, are just...gone, like they were never there to begin with. The woman's voice was my mother's. I should be able to tell her anything. So, when she asked me *"What have you done?"*, I should have answered, *"I'm sorry, Mum, I tried to end my life, I thought you'd understand"*.

Blurred pictures started to come together. I wonder now if this is what people mean when they say your life flashes before your eyes.

It was true, I had tried to kill myself. I had spent last night stocking myself up on painkillers and washing them down with wine and vodka. I had finally come to the conclusion that, not only would the world be better off without me, but that I owed it to those around me to put them out of their misery. I wanted to put myself out of my misery, so I stopped kicking.

*

I remember thinking that morning about the close-minded people of the world who say that people who commit suicide are selfish. Selfish to omit so much pain and sorrow on the people around them who care. At that moment, I thought it was unfair to assume that everyone who commits suicide *has* people who care. Some people don't; perhaps for those people, it is part of the reason they do it in the first place. Perhaps some people end their own suffering only to become a John Doe, an anonymous, tragic victim laying still and empty in a hospital morgue, where nothing much has changed. Where they lie, cold and alone, forever waiting for someone to come to their rescue. No one came to my rescue. To me, it just made sense this way.

It was then that I remembered again, that frantic screaming, those fateful words that will haunt me forever, *"What have you done?"*. And

I had seen my mother's crying face and the fear in her eyes, and I cried, wholeheartedly at the fact that I *am* the most selfish person in the world, and nothing I ever do will take back what I have done. I cry at the fact that in spite of that, nothing has changed, I still wished I was dead.

After leaving the hospital, I felt numb and lifeless, as if I really had died that night. I knew I should feel lucky to still be alive, but I felt nothing. In the first few weeks, I didn't cry, I didn't laugh, I was simply existing. Then one day, I cried. I cried so hard, I thought it would never stop. It was the first time I had been left alone in my mum's house since leaving the hospital and I was enjoying some time alone, listening to music. Then suddenly, without warning, the rest of the world faded into nothing and all that surrounded me was pain. I could feel it pulse through my body like a poison and I cried harder than I'd ever cried in my life. I felt it reach out, wrap itself around my lifeless heart and squeeze until every drop of pain and anger and grief poured from my eye sockets. I thought it would never stop. But when my mum came home and the house came back to life, my tears dried, and I went back to being numb.

The day I tried to kill myself was no different from any other day. In fact, I'd had a good day. I had been at a party in the afternoon. One of those parties where an overly chatty sales rep guilt's you into buying something that you can't afford and that you'll never use. I drank responsibly, I joined conversations with ease, and I laughed with my friends as if nothing was wrong. I enjoyed myself that day for the first time in months. I left, thinking *"OK, I can do this"*.

That day, I had no idea that it would end in A and E. I had no idea that by the end of day, I would have destroyed everything in my path like a tornado, cut every lifeline and hurt beyond repair, every person in my life who had ever really loved me.

When I was out that afternoon, the sun shined, flowers bloomed, and there was laughter and smiles and hope in the air all around me. I breathed it in, I felt it. All the way home, all the way down the street, walking up the stairs to my new flat, I felt it.

But as soon as I closed the door, the light went off. I was left in darkness. Choking, breathless, burning, haunting darkness. It was like hitting a switch. The difference between light and dark, life and death. Here I was again. My day in the sun, laughing and smiling and hoping just made it all the harder, when the laughter stopped. I was moving on, living my life. Yet as soon as I crossed the threshold back into my real life, here I was again. I just couldn't seem to hold on to it. Suddenly, I was overwhelmed by tiredness. I was so tired of being tired. What better to do when you are tired, than to lay down and sleep? If I can't hold on to the good times, if the darkness will always creep back in, no matter what I do, am I going to spend my entire life trying? What kind of life is that? I had fought for years and I had gotten nowhere. So why bother?

After I left Mark and the rest of our friends, I rented my own flat in the same estate, in the next block over. I knew it was a bad idea at the time, I knew that I shouldn't go back there so soon, but I couldn't stop myself. From my top floor window, I could still see everything that went on in my old building, with my old friends. Nothing had changed. After I left, everyone simply went on with their lives, including Mark. I felt like my whole world had ended, and everyone else just kept on going as if nothing was missing. If I did give up, if I really was gone, everyone else would surely just carry on with their own lives, completely unaffected.

I convinced myself that my family would understand. That if they knew for one minute the pain that I was in, had been in for so long, that they would understand. I pictured myself reasoning with them, arguing my case that I had fought a good fight, but you need to know when to stop fighting. Eventually, my mum would sit back, unable to disagree with my logic. She wants more than anything for me to be happy, I know this. I imagined her realising that I had *tried* to be happy and failed. Realising that *this* is the best thing for me. She sits back, defeated *"OK, if this is what you really want"*. I imagined her unwavering motherly love for a child who is suffering. I imagined her agreeing, reluctantly, but out of love, to agree to pull the plug. I decided that night, that she would want me to be at peace. I decided to give up the fight. I decided to kill myself. *"Yes, Mum, this is really what I want"*.

You might imagine that I would have been scared, frantic even, at the prospect of death. You might imagine that people who kill themselves, do so in hysterics. It's not true. Not for me at least. That night, that decision, was the clearest I had ever felt. Once I had made my decision, my mind cleared, like a tranquil sea, a sea of calm. The pressure in my chest deflated, my whole body relaxed. Maybe I was even excited. I would be free. It's all I ever wanted, and I would finally get it. After years of denying myself that relief, I would finally be free. I remember thinking *"I'll even get to see what happens after you die"*. There was no crying, no hysteria, only clarity and relief.

I didn't plan it. But once I had made up my mind, I prepared what would be my perfect last night on earth. I bought my favourite wine, I spent ages choosing just the right music. I changed it several times. Music, I think is the only thing in my life that has ever truly been there for me. It doesn't push, it doesn't judge, it just does. And if it's right, if you let it, it will run through your veins like fire, setting you alight limb for limb. It will move up your spine like electric vines, sending shocks through your body. If there was anything that night that *had* to be just right, it was the music.

After much debate, I chose "Morning View" by Incubus, the album that had helped me through so many hard times in my teenage years. It was the album that I wanted to take to my grave with me. If these would be my final hours on Earth, then let them be filled with serenity, grace and reflection.

The rest of the night is a blur. Most likely in part from the combination of painkillers and vodka that blurred my memory. But perhaps I just didn't want to remember. I remember there was Incubus, and singing, and wine, and vodka, and pills. Then there was shouting, and crying, and blood, and fear. And then there was white.

*

About a month later, I went back to my flat for the first time since leaving it in the middle of the night in the back of an ambulance. After that night, I went back to live at my mum's house. The decision was made for me that I would move back in with Mum and Dylan. Mum said she didn't think it would be good for me to go back there to live again. What she really meant was that she feared that I would not live at all if I went back there. She was probably right. My hatred for myself, for my life and for this world didn't end when I hit the bottom. My desire to end my life didn't leave me when I failed to even do that right. If anything, it grew. It planted roots in my heart and squeezed until every last drop of life dripped out of me and dried into a dark stain against the cold, hard ground. Only my guilt kept me here, like a prisoner in arms.

I had wallowed in my self-built pit of despair for a month. But after deciding to terminate the lease on my flat early, the time eventually came around when I had to revisit another past life. I took the bus to the end of the street. It took all my energy to stop myself from throwing up the entire journey. I stood outside the building for what felt like an hour, holding myself up by the railing to stop my shaking legs from buckling beneath me. I could feel curtains twitching from the flats all around me. My old neighbours, people that I once mistook for friends, they were watching me; I could feel them. I could hear their thoughts; hear their harsh words judging me, condemning me.

'How could she do this?'

'How could she be so selfish?'

'How dare she show her face around here!'

Everyone knew what I did. How could they not? The last time I left here, it was in the back of an ambulance. I wanted to slip away quietly into the night, but that's not what happened. Quiet, calm. I would just slip away without anyone noticing. And those that did notice, I pictured them turning their heads the other way and pretending I was never there in the first place. Considering my unnecessarily dramatic departure, I guessed the latter would be the most likely. I'm sure that's how they preferred it, to pretend like nothing had happened, like I was never here to begin with. Isn't that just the natural reaction people have when something terrible has happened? To turn away and pretend it didn't exist, when something is going on around them that they'd rather not see. Like when someone is in so much pain that they want to kill themselves, but acknowledging that would cause awkwardness and kill the atmosphere.

But now here I was again, invading their perfect lives with more unnecessary drama that they would rather not acknowledge. Their hating stares bore holes straight though me like bullets. The intensity was the only thing that pushed me back into that building. Even a building full of ghosts was better than a street full of demons.

As soon as I opened the door, I felt them. The ghosts. I could feel them all around me. Crawling all over my skin, running up and down my spine. Only it didn't make me shiver, it made me want to scream, scream until all the air rushed out of my body and left me empty and lifeless on the floor. I wanted to scream until every pane of glass in the building shattered and strewed the carpet with the sharp remnants of my broken life. Just as I felt my legs starting to give way, threatening to collapse me to the floor in the doorway, I heard a door open behind me and voices in the hallway. I threw the door shut, blocking out whatever judgement lay on the other side of the door. *I am home, I am safe.* But I wasn't. I was surrounded by the ghosts that I left there a month ago. They were screaming like banshees. They swirled so fast around me it made my head spin. I ran into the bathroom thinking I was going to be sick. The ghosts followed. I sat on the floor with my back against the wall. Images of the last night I spent here flooded my mind.

For the first time, I remembered. This is where I was. I was sitting in this exact spot, when I tried to take my own life. Only the first time I sat here, there were no ghosts and there was no screaming, there was only calm. I remember everything was calm. That night may have ended in chaos, but before that, there was calm. The most calm there had been for a long, long time. For the first time in my life, I felt like everything was clear. Like those people who claim they have had a 'calling' from God to direct them to their righteous path, I had a calling of my own. And my righteous path was clear as day. It was the calm before the storm.

Now the storm had passed, it was time to clean up what was left behind. I worked as quickly as I could to gather up my belongings and get out. If I was ever going to find a way to move on with my life, I had to find a way to deal with these ghosts.

I had spent my entire life running, trying to desperately leave those ghosts behind. But I finally realised that no matter where I went, they would always follow. I had been to the end of the road and back. I had tried to kill myself and I was still just as haunted as I had ever been. Now there was nowhere left to hide. I had to find a way to live with them.

Chapter 20 - The Trick is to Keep Breathing

"Drive away and try to keep smiling. Get a little rock and roll on the radio and go toward all the life there is with all the courage you can find and all the belief you can muster. Be true, be brave, stand. All the rest is darkness." - Stephen King, IT.

Looking Back and Moving On

Moving on is harder than it sounds. At the time, I still couldn't understand what had happened or why, so I had no hope of figuring out how to fix it. So, I didn't try to. I took each day, one day at a time, until enough time had passed that I could do what I always do best; pretend it never happened. Everyone else did the same thing.

It took me many years to figure out what happened that night, why from out of nowhere, I suddenly decided that now was the time. Even now, sometimes I doubt in my mind that I fully understand it all.

Everyone thought it was because of my breakup with Mark. In a way, it was easier just to let them think that. But it was never about him, that much I knew. It was the last straw. The last piece of the puzzle. A puzzle that had been revealing itself to me piece by piece for so many years before. Showing me that this world was not for me, that it never would be. I tried many times to make my own puzzle, where the sun shone, illuminating all the colours of the world, colours that make life worth living. But every time another piece fell into place, it wouldn't show me the sun shining, it showed that in fact, the world was broken, unfixable. And no amount of trying would ever fix that, so why try?

Mark and I broke up a few weeks before it happened. I was distraught. We both were. There were days when I didn't know how I would get through the day without him by my side. We were supposed to get married. We were meant to be together forever. He was meant to be my rock. And for his part, he never faltered. But after years of losing myself, piece by piece to depression, I could barely recognise myself. And despite being with someone who only lived to make me happy, I could still feel myself fading away into nothing. If even love couldn't save me, then really, what hope is there left?

On the night it happened, I don't think I could have answered why. It has taken me until now to figure things out. But it wasn't about him. It was never about him. But now, after so many years of trying to put the pieces together, I am finally starting to see it. It was about this place. I ended up back at *this* place, with no strength to fight it. I thought that love was the key that would finally save me, but I was wrong. Slowly, it crept back in, drip by drip until one day I woke up, choking.

When I met Mark, I thought it was over. I had finally found someone to love because I wanted to make him happy, not myself. I finally felt that I was no longer alone and that with him by my side, I could do anything. I could be the person I had aspired to be my whole life. Steadfast, unwavering. With him by my side, there would be no clouds. And even if one day they appeared, I knew I could fight them.

But when they came, I couldn't fight them. I was *meant* to be stronger. When I realised I wasn't, I knew I never would be.

So I gave up trying and I let myself drown.

*

When I look back over my 'younger' years, it saddens me to think that those years, that should have been my best, turned out to be my darkest, my wonder years, which should have been cherished. But instead, they were shroud in darkness, stalked by a feeling of ever-impending doom that something worse was always around the corner, or on bad days, that it simply couldn't get any worse. I always believed that it was the rest of the world against me and that I was merely a pawn in some evil game sought to destroy me. Now, as an adult, I understand that the world was not out to destroy me, it was making me who I am today.

In the days and weeks following my suicide attempt, I constantly asked why. Why has this happened to me? How could you let this happen to me? I wasn't entirely sure *who* I was asking, but that didn't stop me from needing an answer. I have never been a religious person of any sorts. But I guess I have always believed, or at least wanted to believe, that there was *something* out there, looking out of each and every one of us. Something in the air, all around us, guiding us towards the right path. Call it fate, destiny or simply the dread of being alone in the world. But for me, I felt comfort in at least the idea that we are not completely on our own, that there was always something fighting our corner.

When I woke up in my hospital bed, heart still beating, lower than I had been, even at the point when I thought I had no reason to keep on breathing, my faith had left me. I was more alone than I had ever been. If there really was someone or something supposedly fighting my corner, looking out for me, then how could they let this happen to me? If there was something out there for me, then it had let me drown. I asked and asked, but I never received my answer. What possible reason could there be to allow me to suffer through endless years of infinite darkness, only to force me to keep breathing, even after I made the decision to stop? I was trapped here, with no reason as to why. It is only now, ten years later, that I realise that I did get my answer and I was not left alone.

Six months after my suicide attempt, I would meet the man who would one day become my husband. Now ten years later I am still here, and I am stronger than ever. I didn't know it at the time but the only way, really is up. Sometimes you need to hit rock bottom before you realise just how important it is to find a way to climb back up.

Just as Tom was my everything when I was sixteen, as an adult, my husband Carl, is my sun, moon and stars. It isn't a particularly exciting or even romantic story. In fact, if told wrong, the story of how we came to be together does not put either of us in a good light. Told incorrectly, we both went to a festival, separately, as acquaintances. I arrived at the festival with my boyfriend (who at the time, I believed I was head over heels in love with, just as I always do). But somehow, I left at the end of the festival with Carl instead. Showing me, as leaving my boyfriend high and dry at a festival and running off with another man and Carl, as having stolen another man's girl. This is not the version that we tend to tell people. The alternative version is much nicer and a much truer account of our first date, which involved Carl valiantly rescuing me from the clutches of an evil ex-boyfriend and spending the weekend protecting me from harm. He still reminds me to this day, of all the bands he missed that weekend whilst he was instead, escorting me through fields upon fields of campsites in search of my missing tent, which had mysteriously moved to a different pitch from where I had left it the day before.

My relationship with Carl was not the whirlwind romance that I was used to. We moved slowly and surely, and when I think of our journey together and the strength of our marriage today, I think of the tortoise and the hare – slow and steady wins the race.

"I fell in love the way you fall asleep: slowly, and then all at once." - John Green, The Fault In Our Stars.

Carl and I spent almost two years dating casually without any predetermined path to our future, no expectations and no judgement. It is the first relationship I have been in that I haven't relied on to hold me up. Every other relationship up till now has ended in disaster, after not being able to live up to the complete and utter dependence that I believed I needed to be whole. When I met Carl, I was at a point in my life where I knew that if I didn't learn to stand on my own two feet, without the crutch of a partner, that I might never learn to stand at all. Having come from one failed relationship to another and another, without ever having the chance to breathe in between, I started our relationship filled with doubt and anxiety, knowing that another man, another romantic disaster, would put me right back to where I was before. Only next time around, I might not be strong enough to come back from it.

But there was something about Carl, something deep and real. Something inside me told me that if I didn't give this a chance, I would regret it for the rest of my life. Now I understand better, that that voice inside of me was telling me that I had found the man I would spend the rest of my life with. Carl, reluctant to leave his bachelor status behind, shared my fears of co-dependence, so we compromised, both agreeing to a slow, causal relationship without any preconceptions, that may or may not grow of its own accord, in its own time. And grow it did. Eventually we came to live together and were very much in love, not a whirlwind love, but a more natural love that grew out of admiration and respect for each other rather than dependency. But I quickly felt my search of independence fading. I wasn't ready to give up the fight to find my own person, so I left. But in the year that we spent apart, we learnt how to live apart, as well as together, forming the basis for a marriage that stands tall today.

For the first time in my life, I am with someone, not because I need to be, but because I choose to be. All I ever wanted was for someone to walk alongside me as I walked on my own two feet. Everyone, no matter how strong, will have times in their lives when they need to be carried, just until they learn how to walk again.

But as much as we all love a fairy-tale ending, meeting Carl did not make all my problems go away; quite the contrary. I had met an amazing man and we were well on track for falling into lifelong love. And instead of enjoying what would also become an important time of my life which should be cherished, I continued to struggle to find a reason to live. The persistence of my problems, even when life should have been good, made me feel all the more hopeless. Claustrophobic in my own skin, I did what I always do, I ran. This has been my natural reaction all my life. I've always run, leaving everything and everyone behind. I guess I always thought that I could leave my problems behind too, but somehow, they always followed and eventually, it would be time to run again. And once more, it *was* time to run again. But now, I felt like I had reached the point of no return. Running away from my problems had never worked in the past and now, they ran so deep that I knew they would come with me. So that's what I did. I took them with me. And for the first time in my life, I did not try to quash them. I did not try to fix them. I wore them like scars, battle wounds. I took them halfway across the world to South Africa. I had to find a place for them, to find a way that we could live together in acceptance. I had to be alone with my problems to let myself feel them, to really get to know them. And alone with my problems, I learned how to mix dark with light and how to live in harmony with my past. In doing that, I found not only peace with my past, but I came to understand the person I had become because of it.

I spent several months in a place more diverse than I could have ever imagined in my wildest dreams. South Africa is beautiful and barren, tranquil and full of hate, rich and poor, simple and complex. I had no idea that one place, one experience, could be so many things all at one time, all working together to become the great diverse nation that we see today. It didn't have to be dark or light, it could be both. People don't have to be happy or struggling, they could learn to be both.

When I first arrived in Cape Town, I had no idea what kind of effect this country would have on me. I came to South Africa to be somewhere else, to be outside of my own life for a while, to do something that I was actually choosing to do, rather than something I needed to do. The first part of my trip I considered recuperation. I made new friends, I drank cocktails, sunbathed, shopped and got to spend my days working with injured penguins (that's right, there are penguins in South Africa!). I had a blast, but nothing had changed. In the second part of my trip, I left the comfort of my suburban bunkbed and went out to see the world. During my travels, I began reading Nelson Mandela's *The Road to Freedom*. In it, he writes of the relentless struggle of the apartheid. Of losing battle after battle but never losing faith, never losing hope that one day, the war will be won and sun will shine once more upon South Africa. I was touched by the strength and determination of the apartheid freedom fighters, and although I couldn't possibly compare my own darkness to the oppression of an entire nation, it did make me think of my own battles and the wars that I had faced and lost, and those that I had won. I may be struggling to find a reason to keep breathing, but I was doing just that, breathing. If I can find nothing else to be thankful for, I can at least be thankful for that.

And then one night, without any warning I found a reason. I watched, as the colour slowly trickled back into my vision. And when I looked again, this time, it was in colour. And I saw that the world could truly be a beautiful and magical place.

The day that everything changed, I remember it like it was yesterday. Carl had joined me for a short time during my trip and we travelled together to a remote village on the south east coast of South

Africa called Coffee Bay. It was like nothing I had ever seen before. Even as we trundled up the dirt roads towards the village, we passed a rusted old jeep, bursting at the seams with local men. They were laughing and joking and singing along to the music that blasted out. They filled the cab and the cargo area like canned sardines, and they were even sitting on the roof of the cab, gripping to the roof racks as the truck threw them about on the bumpy road. Could you ever image such a scene in the UK? Imagine the uproar about road safety and careless driving they would cause! But here, the attitude is more along the lines of *'well, what's the worst that could happen?'*.

The village itself was remotely scattered with mud-huts with straw roofs and no coverings on the windows or doors. The larger houses were composed of corrugated metal sheets, separated by drapes of colourful fabrics. Women sat on the dirt ground outside their houses with metal pots between their knees, preparing dinner for their families. The one shop in the village was a portacabin with no more than 30 commercial products for sale, to service the entire community. We passed children by the side of road who stopped to stare and wave at us through the bus windows, dressed in rags and shoeless, with swollen, malnourished belly's and ribs that you could count by sight. When we stepped out of the bus, all the children ran over to see us. Another group of privileged white tourists in our Nike shoes and Superdry t-shirts and expensive digital cameras, come to experience another world, while the children were doing the same to us. I was amazed to realise just how much 'stuff' we think we need to make us happy. But these children, they had nothing. And yet the smiles we saw on their faces that day, were some of the most genuine smiles I had seen in my life. They smiled and laughed at us, they reached out wanting to touch our hands, happy to welcome us to their home.

These people suffer greatly from real problems; poverty, famine, drought, malnutrition. Not to mention the insufferably high mortality rate in children, as well as adults from deadly infections such as malaria and HIV. These are problems that they can't fix, not alone anyway. They can't turn around and look at their lives and think *'No, this isn't working for me. I need to do something to make this better"*. This is the way they live, and they have learnt to do just that, to play with the cards that life dealt them. And when you see the shining smiles of the children as they chase after the few cars that pass through their bare village, when you see the excitement in their eyes and in their laughter that new people have arrived for them to experience, to talk to and to touch, you would think that these children had never seen a hard time in their lives. So, if these poverty-stricken, malnourished and starving children can be genuinely happy to run around bare footed, happy just to be alive, then can't I learn to be happy with the life that I had been given? That day in Coffee Bay made me realise just how thankful I should be for how my life turned out. Not everyone has as much as I do to be thankful for.

Later that afternoon, the boys that passed us earlier in the jeep came to our hostel to collect all the 'visitors' for a bonfire. We all piled into the back of the jeep and again, the surplus guys sat on the roof (the locals, not the tourists). They took us down to the beach where another group of local guys were just getting a fire started, just in time for the sun going down. As we sat around enjoying the heat from the fire in the quickly cooling evening, the local boys sang us songs and played African bongo drums with such passion and such rhythm that I wondered if their heartbeats synchronised to the beat of the drum. I watched one boy, not even a teenager, drum along with the others. I saw him transport into another time and place, like it was him and drum, and there was nothing else in the entire world; he was mesmerising. I would give anything to be so completely content as he was in the moment. But then, as I took in the rest of my surroundings, the energising beat of the drums, the harmonic African song, the captivating beauty of the fire, the roar of the ocean behind me and my favourite person in the world, arm around my shoulders, I realised, I was. I was content. I was more than content. I was seeing everything in colour. Bright, vibrant, captivating colour and it was absolutely beautiful. The *world*, was beautiful. Just as I always knew that it was. That was all I needed. All this time, all I ever really wanted to know, was that it was all worth it.

And even now, ten years on, every time I smell the burning wood in the warm summer air, or I hear the ocean roaring in time with the breeze in the air, I'm transported straight back to that moment on the beach at Coffee Bay, the happiest moment of my life, and I am reminded to be thankful that I kept breathing long enough to realise that I still wanted to.

Do Unto One Another

"How wonderful it is that nobody need wait a single moment before starting to improve the world." – Ann Frank.

My past is what gets me through the days. Knowing that I'm not a failure, I'm a survivor. Knowing that I am grateful to be alive, and that I *want* to be alive. Once, I almost wasn't alive and I had no will to live. Recently, a friend of mine took his own life. He too, lost his will to live. Dan was one of the kindest, most genuine people I have met in a long time. I know that everyone says that of someone they knew that passed away, but I've honestly never known anyone to leave such a lasting impression, after knowing them for such a short time. We weren't particularly close, in fact, I guess I didn't even know him that well, but what I do know is that this world would be unbearable without the selflessness and kindness of people, people just like Dan.

During my final year of university, I was offered a summer placement in a state-of-the-art research facility that any other student in my position would give their right arm for. It was in Glasgow. A city famous for stabbings, random muggings and people being murdered in bars for wearing the wrong football colours. As much as I wanted the placement, I was terrified! I was a country girl moving to the big city, and I was doing it alone! Carl's brother and some of his friends lived in the city, so I was grateful to be able to stay with them for the summer during my placement, but I was still essentially alone. Carl took me down to Glasgow and helped me move in, but then, he went home to Aberdeen. I was so scared. The minute Carl left, all I wanted to do was run after him. I know I've been away, alone before, but it really doesn't get any easier. That first afternoon alone in the house, I hid in my room, determined I would spend the next three months miserable, the only girl in a house of five boys, only one of which I even remotely knew, and at risk of a gang shooting every time I left the house to go to a job that by now, I'd convinced myself that I was going to be shit at anyway!

Within half an hour of sulking on my bed came a knock on my door, followed by a smiling face and a steaming cup of tea.

"Hello. Thought you might like a brew."

A genuine smile and a simple welcoming gesture and suddenly, everything was going to be alright.

That weekend, Dan took me into the town centre to show me how to get between the different bus stops I would need for my commute and to show me his favourite shops. When he took me to *"stuff"* we realised we shared a common interest: junk!

He helped me orientate myself through a maze of city centre people-traffic and even quizzed me to make sure I knew how to get back home if I got turned around. I remember he used a huge digital billboard as a landmark, so if I got lost, I could walk around the grid of streets until I found the *"got milk?"* sign, then I would know which way was up.

"See? As long as you've got Mr T, and he's got milk, you'll never get lost!"

And he was right.

After I told him I didn't know exactly where the institute was, he insisted we do a trial run and took a bus with me across the city and back again to find out, a three-hour round trip. One day with Dan, and I loved my new city. I wasn't afraid, I wasn't alone, I was home and I was welcome.

When I first heard about Dan's death, nothing happened. When Carl first told me, my initial response was, *"Oh. I really liked Dan"*. I think I've had more dramatic responses to TV shows being cancelled. At the time, when Carl's mum called to tell us, I was on my way out the door to a body combat class. Always on the lookout for a valid excuse not to have to go to the gym, I remember thinking, *"This, seems like a good enough reason to skip Combat tonight"* and I went about making myself a cup of tea instead. It wasn't until about 24 hours later, 24 hours after hearing that Dan had killed himself, that I felt a huge, wholehearted and completely unexpected punch in the stomach, knock all the breath from my body. It's the only way I can describe it, like a punch in the stomach. It hit over and over again, increasing the frequency until eventually I was left with the constant feeling that I was going to vomit. For weeks. I thought of nothing but him. Every time I closed my eyes, I would see his smiling face, peeking around my bedroom door. I would see the excited look in his eyes whenever someone suggested watching *The Wire*. And I saw the complete selflessness in him, when he spent the entire day just trying to make me feel welcome.

One of the memories that I think about the most, is *"The Ant War"*. Carl had come down for the weekend and we had spent the day together in the city. The moment we came through the front door to the house, Dan's wild, excited face was in front of us, like he had been waiting behind the door to jump out like a crazy person onto whoever came through it first.

"I'm so glad you're home!"

Excitement beamed from him like a madman!

"It's happening again! You have to see this!"

He darted back into the house like a wild thing, leaving Carl and I speechless in the doorway. Ordinarily, Dan is quite a subdued, deep thinking kind of character. So, to see him running about like a kid at

Christmas came as a bit of a surprise!

Carl and I shrugged and followed.

When we came to the back door, he was crouched down, his arms hugging his knees, staring into the patio.

"Is…is everything OK?"

I worried that he had *actually* gone mad.

"Look closer."

His eyes never left the patio. Carl and I stepped forward towards where Dan was staring into nothing. But it wasn't nothing. He wasn't looking at the patio. He was watching the hundreds, thousands of ants, scattering aimlessly all over the patio.

"Oh wow!"

"No," he corrected. "Just wait."

His eyes still glued to the patio, I crouched down next to him and joined him, not quite sure what else I was waiting for and still a little concerned for Dan's sanity. Suddenly, a fly, twice the size of the ant, swooped down and attacked the company. But it didn't carry away the helpless ant like I expected. Instead, it was swarmed by the hundreds of ants around it. Another fly attacked, and then another, and the same thing happened over and over again. The flies came in their dozens, more and more of them. The entire patio had turned into a battle zone. Everywhere I looked, there were swarms of ants devouring the flying insects twice their body weight and carrying them off on their backs into the cracks between the slabs of concrete.

"It's a war! An *ant* war!"

After about half an hour the flies retreated. The ants won the war. The little man, the underdog, against all odds, coming out on top. It really was a glorious scene. If you think about it, it really isn't much different with people. Isn't it amazing what can be achieved when we work together? When we are there for one another.

Sometimes, when I think about Dan, it makes me smile, grateful to have such great memories of a truly unforgettable person. But most of the time, when I close my eyes, I don't see the happy memories that make me smile. I see his pain. I *feel* his pain. I see him distraught, knowing that there is nothing left. I feel his terror rushing through my blood and tensing every muscle in my body, knowing that his death is coming. I see him fighting invisible demons, demons that are whispering to him that this is the only way. I can feel every breath of his pain because I've been there once myself. But when I think about the night that I wanted everything to end, it didn't scare me, it calmed me. I didn't feel pain or fear, I felt relief that it was almost over. I wonder if Dan was in pain, if he was scared? Or was he calm? Was he more peaceful than he had ever been in his life, knowing that soon it would be over, that he wouldn't have to fight anymore? Was he tired like I was? Wanting nothing more than to simply go to sleep and never wake up.

Dan's funeral was the most horrendous event I have ever attended. There must have been 200 people there, most of whom were under 30. The minister tried hard to turn it into a celebration of Dan's life. But it didn't change the fact that he was stood in front of 200 people, whose lives would forever be emptier now that Dan wasn't in them. As I looked around at my brother-in-law and his friends, I grieved not only for Dan, but for them. Grown men crying publicly, at the best friend they had lost. I saw Dan's family. His mum, his dad, his sister, all distraught. I grieved for them, losing their son, their brother. But as I watched how Dan's death had devastated an entire family, I selfishly thought of my own. I had come so close to doing this exact thing to them. I almost ripped them apart. Dan's family will never recover from this. And mine would have been no different. If I had died that night, even now, ten years on, my family would still be broken. I always knew what I had done or tried to do. I always knew the pain that I had caused my family by what I did that night; it's something I will never forgive myself for. But it took witnessing it first hand, witnessing how the death of a beloved family member, and more particularly the suicide of a family member, can rip so many people apart, all at once.

If I have learned one thing in my whole life, it is to be thankful. Things could have turned out so differently and I am so thankful that they didn't. Afterwards, I felt more pain than I ever thought imaginable. Sometimes I still do. But I will take every moment of that pain, just to prevent my family from ever going through what Dan's family did. But it's not all pain. There is good in the world and the world is a beautiful place, full of beautiful people.

*

Sometimes, it's the little things that count. Recently, my brother wrote a post on Facebook that I have no doubt brought a smile to the faces of each and every person who read it. My brother is not a sentimental person by any means, but the kindness of strangers can touch us all. This is what he wrote:

"Night absolutely made! Standing at the bus stop and an old guy walking past with his wee dog shouts "Heymin! Got a ticket yet?" I reply, "No I don't usually take the bus". Straight off he replies, "here you go" and hands me a day ticket from today. What an awesome but simple gesture. Gonna pass this on to the first person I see at the bus stop once I get off."

It might only be a bus ticket, but the smile that the gesture created, is priceless.

Everyone has a story like Dylan's.

Unsolicited kindness touches our hearts in more ways than we can imagine. And what's more, it inspires us to share that kindness, to choose to make someone else smile in the same way that a stranger chose to make us smile. You don't need to be depressed to appreciate a little bit of kindness. In a world that can be so harsh, and cruel, and unforgiving, we should all being doing *something* to make each other smile. It really is the simple things in life that make us smile. And when they do make you smile, pass it on. Remember that you have a reason to smile; maybe the person you will pass when getting off the bus this morning, or the person walking unprotected in a downpour, or lost and alone in the big city, may still be looking for theirs.

Be the reason someone smiles today.

*

As much as it's important to be kind to one another, don't forget to show yourself some kindness too. Sometimes, you have to look after yourself, you have to be there for yourself. You could wait forever for someone to hold out their hand to you, not because people don't care, but because people are not mind readers. If you do not ask for a hand to hold, then how will anyone ever know that you need one? And that part's up to you; to do that for yourself. Believe it or not, there are people out there waiting to hold your hand, waiting to help you back from the ledge. It's probably one of the hardest things I have done, in all the years I have let myself fade away through depression; bringing myself back to life, just enough to ask someone for help; to ask someone to care. But they are out there, and when you are strong enough, one day you will find them for yourself. And when you do find them, the whole world will change. One day, you will remember that the world is not immersed in shadow. You will remember that the world is full of beautiful colours and beautiful people. You will remember that there is still kindness in the world; in the eyes of your friends and family and in the eyes of the strangers that pass you by every day on the street.

Interesting fact of the day: 1 in 4 people suffer mental health problems. Imagine, being in a room with 100 people. As a depressive, you feel alone, the only one, like there is something wrong with you. But while you are alone in a room with 100 other people, 24 of them feel exactly the same way you do. We don't say it out loud, but that doesn't make it any less true. You may feel completely alone, but it doesn't mean that you are. This is the thought that gets me through each day. I wonder what difference it would have made to me at seventeen when I was alone and delusional, or at twenty-one when I finally gave up on life. Would knowing this have saved my life? If I had spoken out to that room of 100 people, if I had been strong enough to ask for help, would someone have reached out to me and helped me back from the ledge? Everyone, no matter how strong or stubborn, needs to know sometimes that the world is not against them and that they are not alone.

Recently I read a book written by a woman who suffered severe depression. After years of repressing my own emotions, the brutal honesty and openness of her writing made me feel anxious and uncomfortable. One chapter she wrote made me cry. Like a lightbulb illuminating, I felt an overwhelming relief at finding that my complex ideas that I have not even begun to fully understand myself, ideas that had not even been found yet, were shared by someone else. To see them written on the pages in front of me; to feel such a connection with a person that I had never met, split me at the seams; my heart poured out in thankfulness.

*

We live in a chaotic world. Every person on this planet has days where the world moves too fast; days where we struggle to keep our footing. It is important to find a way to keep yourself grounded. For me, it is writing and music. Writing is a release without judgement. No one can hear me do it, no one ever has to see it, but it is still out there. Silently unburdening me. Writing, and seeing my emotions written down in front of me, helps me to understand them and helps me to give them some perspective. Sometimes the problems in my mind, they seem so big. But when I see them written down, suddenly they feel so much smaller. I guess the same reason why many people find it easier to talk to a stranger rather than a friend, and why the times I do open up to those around me, I do it with the lights off, in darkness, when no one can see me. Anonymously.

But sometimes it is hard to find the words. Sometimes you don't know what they are or what you need them to be. Sometimes, we can't know, or see the truth, until it is told to us. Music will always tell us the truth. Music is the anthem to our lives, to ourselves at that particular moment in time and will forever be assigned to that moment, to that memory. Music can help us to remember not only who we once were, but who we are constantly striving to be. When we feel alone, it can remind us that in fact, we are not. When we feel that nobody could possibly understand what we are going through, the pain that we are in each and every day, music can show us that actually, there are people out there that do understand. It can remind us that you are not the only person in the world who has ever felt pain. And most importantly, music can remind us that although you may be feeling pain right now, one day you will come through it and find that the sun is shining on the other side. Music reminds us that the sun is worth fighting for and that when we are forced to learn how to fight, we become stronger.

Music can act as our memories. It can remind us of another time, a happier time. Maybe it will remind us of a rough time. A time that when we look back on now, it shows us how much stronger we are today. It can remind us that sometimes we have to go through these tough times to allow us to become the people we are today. And although at the time it was hell, you would not be the person you are today without it. Our memories, good or bad can ground us, back to the person we became, because of the things we have experienced.

Make Yourself

"After one has been in prison, it is the small things that one appreciates: being able to take a walk whenever one wants, going into a shop and buying a newspaper, speaking or choosing to remain silent. The simple act of being able to control one's person." - Nelson Mandela.

Now all these years on, it amazes me to think back to my world then and the person that I once was. I think of the person that I am today, and I am unrecognisable to that girl back then. I have completely transformed, and it amazes me that I was able to find within myself, the power to do so. Now, I am independent, and I am strong, stronger than I would have ever imagined I could have been.

I watched a film recently that followed a family of survivors in the aftermath of the 2004 tsunami that destroyed so many lives across Southeast Asia. The story tried to show us that when times test us, we can stand to be tested, that we are stronger than we know and that sometimes it takes darkness, to show us the light. The character that spoke to me the most was the family's son, a young boy who at the beginning of the film, was just that, a young boy. In the wake of the disaster, we watched as the boy flourished into a strong, brave man who held the rest of his family together. The tsunami forced him to stand up and take control of the situation, and he found in himself an impeccable strength that he didn't know he had. The boy's transformation made me think about where I have come from and how my story has shaped me into the person I am today.

Many would say that it is the trials and tragedies that we encounter through life that allow people to find their inner potential, a sort of emotional evolution, if you will. It has taken a long time for me to get to where I am now, but I do believe that it is the things I have experienced in my life, that have led me here.

Of course, my story does not involve a major tragedy. There are so many other people out there that have suffered a far greater loss than any that I could even imagine. My tragedy was not a physical, life-shattering event to the likes of the tsunami, it was an emotional one, and the loss that I suffered, was the loss of myself. It has taken many years, but now in adulthood, I have finally found myself. I could say that *this* is the person that I should have been all along, that the darkness I lived in all my life stopped me from being this person. I struggled for so long, desperately trying to get to who I was *meant* to be, but maybe I wasn't *meant* to be anyone, maybe it was all just part of the journey. I believe now that the rough times and the darkness I endured in my teenage years, has made me the adult I am today. I often wonder, if things had been different, if I hadn't been attacked, if I hadn't spiralled out of control, if I hadn't tried to take my own life, would I still be this person today? My teenage years were the worst of my life and I wouldn't wish my experience on anyone; but at the same time, I wouldn't change them for the world. Of course, there will always be things I would have done differently. I wouldn't have hurt my family the way that I did. I wouldn't have pushed them away when I'm sure if I had let them, they would have been there to help me though this. Instead, I made them another set of faces in an anonymous sea of people that silently passed through my life. But regrets or not, the experience of living with depression has made me a stronger person than I ever would have become without it, an or that, I am truly grateful. I hope that my family will also find some solace here, that they will understand that everything that happened to me, or that I let happen, was a necessary evil that helped me to flourish into an adult that I can respect. Back then, I never would have thought it was possible for me to be this way, to be brave and to be strong and to know that if I can come through the other side of depression, if I can claw back my will to live, I can do anything.

I recently had a conversation with a work colleague about just this and I will forever be grateful to her for helping me come to this realisation and showing me that I do have the strength to carry on, even if some days still, it doesn't seem that way. She spoke of her own personal trials and the ways in which she has taught herself to be strong. She runs. She runs to keep herself pushing forward, to remind herself of her capabilities and of the pain she once fought and won. She told me that she runs for the pain, to remind herself of her survival, motivating her to keep pushing forward through the pain. Conquering that pain makes her feel like she can achieve anything and reminds her that, even though somethings might always be painful, things will never be as bad as they once were. She runs to stop herself from becoming complacent, to remember that in comparison to the pain she once suffered, the little things in life that we so often let under our skin simply don't matter.

I have been trying to finish this chapter for many years now. I have written and rewritten so many times, at different points of my life, trying to find my happy ending. I wanted to end on a high. To show you, and to show myself, that although I have lived a lot of my life in darkness, there is another side, and the grass is greener. But the reason why the green is so green, is because it wasn't always. But trying to end a book on a high or low point is impossible. Life is transient; and in survival stories, such as I consider this to be, there is no end point. But maybe it's not about the happy ending, maybe it's about the happiness we can find on the way. Maybe we will never consider ourselves to have found that happy ending, maybe we will keep forever searching for it. But surely, if you are still looking, then you still believe there can be one?

One thing I do know for sure is that it was the darkness that pressed down on me and moulded and shaped me into the person I am today. I am stronger, and I am thankful that I stand here today, feeling the heat from the once-hidden sun kiss my cheeks. When everything is good, I write of the sun shining and wind blowing and that everything is as it should be. But that is not always the case; even for the shiniest people on this planet, that is not always the case. On other days, it seems that the sun does not shine, and the wind does not blow. But even on the darkness days, at least now I know that the trick is to keep breathing, because one day the sun will shine again, and when it returns, it will be brighter than ever before.

I know now that it will return. And because of the darkness that I have faced throughout my life, I know how to survive until it does.

It is our experiences and what we make of them that make us the people that we are today. We make ourselves.

MAKE YOURSELF

About the Author

Throughout her life, Gillian struggled with depression and anxiety. In a time before we had ever heard the terms 'depression' or 'mental stigma', she suffered in silence, afraid to tell anyone of the darkness clouding her mind, in fear that she would be labelled as crazy. When the depression followed her into adulthood, she stopped trying to outrun it and accepted it with open arms into her life, as part of herself, and the driving force behind the person she has become today. During her darker moments, she found solace in the pages of empty notebooks, where she deepest and darkest thoughts, the premise for what would one day become her first book. Writing her story gave her great therapy and helped her to see the path to acceptance. She hopes that by passing on her 'words of wisdom' it may be some small help to others suffering from mental illness, by showing them that they are not alone and that there is no need to be afraid. Gillian has dreamt for years of being able to call herself an author and hopes that one day she will find the time to finish some of the other stories that have been started, but not finished over the years!

For more information about our books,
or our publishing services, please visit
www.green-cat.co

Printed in Great Britain
by Amazon